Pleasures *of the* Porch

Pleasures *of the* Porch

IDEAS FOR GRACIOUS OUTDOOR LIVING

DARIA PRICE BOWMAN ❦ MAUREEN LaMARCA

RIZZOLI
NEW YORK

First published in the United States of America in 1997 by
Rizzoli International Publications, Inc.
300 Park Avenue South, New York, N.Y. 10010

LC 96-70340
ISBN 0-8478-2005-X

Pleasures of the Porch
was prepared and produced by
Michael Friedman Publishing Group, Inc.
15 West 26th Street
New York, New York 10010

Editor: Susan Lauzau
Art Director: Lynne Yeamans
Designer: Andrea Karman
Photography Editor: Wendy Missan
Production Manager: Camille Lee

Color separations by Fine Arts Repro House Co., Ltd.
Printed in Singapore by KHL Printing Co Pte Ltd.

Dedicated with love to my husband Ernie Bowman who,
once upon a time, perfected the art of porch sitting.

Thanks go to my wonderful daughters, Sam and Cassie, who are patient and understanding even when I'm on yet another deadline. To my parents, Elizabeth and Carl Price, for their confidence in me and my work. And to Larry Keller for his willingness to share with me his extraordinary knowledge of antique garden furniture.

DBP

For Aunt Sue

Thanks to the Master Gardeners of Hunterdon County, Carolyn and Joe Puleo of The City Store, the staff at the reference department of the Hunterdon County Regional Library, Nathalie Monahan, Joanne Rajoppi, and Sal, Susan, and Rebecca.

ML

Contents

Above: a quiet approach is taken on this beautifully sedate porch. Here, a simple country bench is placed at the perfect angle to watch the setting sun.

Left: This lovingly decorated wrap-around evokes a sense of comfort and tradition. The porch's conventional colors on ceiling and floor are accented by mustard-colored walls and accessories in sunny yellows and cool blues, a favorite color combination in the picturesque farmhouses of Provence. The table set in shade is a perfect spot for a light lunch of cold salads, while the round table at the sun-washed far end of the porch offers a cheerful place to read the morning paper over coffee or to play board games with the family late into the summer evenings.

Introduction

The very idea of a porch evokes vivid, nostalgic images from our collective memory. We recall family life from an earlier, slower-paced era—a time before computers and fax machines, before "workaholics" and bicoastal lifestyles. When we think of the porch, we see Mother in an apron shelling peas in preparation for Sunday dinner. There's Grandfather telling tall tales to a rapt group of children.

Successful decorating is all in the details, and porch decor is no different. A simple brick Victorian house with a well-proportioned front porch is packed with whimsical and clever details that point to the owner's creativity and delightful sense of humor. Eclectic furnishings include lyre-backed chairs and matching daybed and porch swing, along with a charming elephant-shaped child's chair. Marble-topped plant stands, a cast-iron urn holding a magnificent staghorn fern, and an elaborate metal candelabra allude to the Victorian heritage of the porch. The arrangement, while cluttered, avoids being too busy with the unifying use of white and shades of blue in the cotton runner on the floor and the fabrics covering the many pillows. An unusual and attractive touch is the oval metal-framed mirror placed between the windows to reflect the light from the candles.

If we listen carefully, we can hear the cheerful tinkle of ice in a pitcher of fresh lemonade, the slow, steady creak of a rocking chair, and the giggles of pigtailed girls playing tea party with their dolls. The romantic in us can visualize a young couple courting on the porch swing while an anxious father peers out through the screened door. And we can feel the cool breath of the breeze as it keeps the oppressive heat of summer at bay.

Porches were, at first, a functional part of a dwelling, built to shelter the interior from extreme cold and heat. Porch popularity continued to grow, climaxing with the excesses and exuberance of the Victorian period and ultimately waning when people moved indoors to the family room and the television or out to the backyard, with its patio and barbecue. Many of the old Victorian porches were stripped off for maintenance purposes, and siding replaced clapboard as suburban living evolved.

Today, the porch is experiencing a resurgence in popularity. Some observers say it's part of a nostalgic trend and others say it's purely psychological—bound up with our need to reduce stress and simplify our lives. Whatever the sociological causes, since the 1980s, porch additions, new construction, and restorations (many taking years, reconstructing with painstaking accuracy the intricate gingerbread work found on the original) are on the rise.

Since the greater part of our day is often spent cooped up in offices where the air quality is poor and windows are at a premium, it's little wonder that the idea of sitting out on a porch in the fresh air is so attractive. A porch is an inviting, comfortable place to spend leisure time, and with so little time to spare from busy work lives, more and more families are committing themselves to creating an outdoor haven where they can relax and restore their equilibrium.

Flowers and porches are made to be together. A small but color-packed bed of annuals—marigolds, petunias, salvia, and marguerites—frames the wraparound porch of a gothic-inspired bungalow. More blooms, these in pretty ceramic cache pots, extend the floral theme to the porch floor, where a rag rug in pastel tones defines a seating space. Ornate wicker and layers of vintage linens complement the fancy shingle siding.

Whether you are thinking about building a porch or simply about making better use of the porch you've got, this book will help you consider all the possibilities for planning and decorating this outdoor space. Once you've decided on the type of porch that best suits your family, discuss your needs thoroughly with an architect or builder. For example, if dining is a priority, a porch built close to the kitchen would be ideal. If privacy and quiet time are priorities, you might want to tuck a smaller porch into the side of your house or up on a second level off a bedroom. But if neighborliness is important to you and you'd like to encourage visiting, think about building your porch on the front of the house. Porches also make ideal outdoor playrooms; if you plan to use your porch as a place for children to romp, build it as wide and long as local permits allow.

Above: The best porches serve many purposes. Dining alfresco under a protective roof is one of the porch's most charming uses. A rustic stone chimney wall dictates the style of this shaded porch, where the dining table—set with picnic fixings—is made of rough-hewn logs.

Right: In the charming style of southwestern haciendas, this porch has been constructed of timber and adobe. Consider well the style of the house before committing to a porch plan. The porch should complement and enhance the house's facade, rather than contrast jarringly with the prevailing style.

The Porch's Past

Whether it's called a piazza, portico, loggia, veranda, gallery, stoop, or even an ombra, the porch brings to mind thoughts of a relaxed retreat, summer nights, and country simplicity.

How did porches evolve?

Architectural historians suggest that the earliest porches were the rocky overhangs of cave dwellings. We know a little more about the Greek *porticus*—a columned entryway to a temple or public building—from which our word "porch" is derived. These structures typically consisted of two columns that supported a pointed roof, and provided a proper transition between interior and exterior. During the Middle Ages, porticos evolved into covered vestibules in northern European cathedrals and into arcaded loggias in Italian cities.

It wasn't until much later that porches graced residential buildings. And they came to us by way of the tropical locales of India and the West Indies. A British trade paper dated 1711 describes an Indian building as being "very ancient, two stories high, and has...two large Verandas or Piazzas." Another description from 1757 describes "a penthouse or shed that forms what is called in the Portuguese Lingua *Verandas*, [which are] either round, or on particular sides of the house." Other eighteenth-century accounts spell the word "verander," "voranda," "virander," "feranda," and "feerandah." By about 1800, the English were regularly using the new and exotic word "verandah" to describe what we think of today as a porch.

At about same time the English were learning about porch living from their tropical colonial outposts, Flemish and Dutch settlers in the New World were building houses with overhanging eaves. The

The prototype for centuries of porches, the south portico of the Erechtheum on the Acropolis in Athens was built around 421 to 413 B.C. The best-known features of this portico are the six caryatids—stone columns fashioned into female figures—that support the heavy stone roof. These beautiful sculptures inspired many copies, especially by the ancient Romans, some of which can be found in the Forum and Hadrian's Villa in Rome. Today, the original caryatids live in the Acropolis Museum in Athens. The figures shown here are reproductions.

Above: Though we tend to think of porches in rural and small town settings, urban examples abound. Wrought-iron porches with elaborate filigree designs appear in duplicate and triplicate on these city streets. The heights of these "galeries" hint at the lofty ceilings of the dwellings, while the depth indicates the designer's intention to keep the interior spaces cool.

Above right: A wide cornice, heavily detailed supporting braces, and intricately decorative balustrades adorn this two-story porch set in a lush, nearly tropical garden. Architectural details as rich as these sometimes originated in the pattern books that were widely circulated in the nineteenth century.

Flemish, who settled first in southern Holland and then in North America on the western end of Long Island, called the overhanging eaves "flying gutters," and their purpose was purely practical—they protected the fragile lime and straw walls of these early houses, whose style is now known as Dutch Colonial. Later, flared roof lines became popular, and the overhang served as the roof of the porch, with a platform below and colonnettes supporting the overhang.

In French Colonial Quebec, houses were built with the eaves flaring out to form a porch roof, similar to those of the Flemish and Dutch settlers. The Québécois called the flared eave a "galerie," and these galeries have a common origin to the wrought-iron examples found a few years later in New Orleans.

In the American South, as well as in the Caribbean, Australia, and other warm climates, houses were built with deep, two-story porches all the way around the exterior. These wraparound porches protected the walls of the house, allowed windows to remain open in inclement weather, and most importantly, shaded interiors from the fierce summer sun.

Spanish settlers and missionaries, who began to establish communities in the Southwest in the early 1600s, also included porches in their construction. The Palace of the Governors in Santa Fe, New Mexico, built in 1610 and still standing today, has a two-story loggia that not only protects the adobe walls, but also provides deep shade for the interior.

The gracious Georgian (1730–1820) period of architecture in North America paid homage to the latest style in England, while Federal style (1790-1815) celebrated the promise of the new American nation. Symmetry and classical details were the home-building watchwords of the day. Porches grew from gabled overhangs to columned and pedimented porch hoods to domed circular porticos. Soon, porches became perfectly proportioned pedimented gable ends supported by columns.

The Greek Revival period, from 1820 to 1860, brought an adaptation of Classical Greek temple designs to the front facades of houses. Grand porticos with pediments supported by columns graced even tiny, two-room houses. Nearly every town with a few homes from this period can boast at least one Greek Revival relic.

In 1837, Victoria became Queen of England, establishing a reign that would last for the better part of the century, till her death in 1901. During this era, known to us as the Victorian age, a variety of styles emerged and receded. Often grouped together as Victorian, they are as diverse as Gothic Revival, Italianate, Queen Anne, Second Empire, and Shingle and Stick styles.

One of the best-known porches is at George Washington's Mount Vernon in Virginia. In 1787, he added a mammoth two-story open porch supported by graceful columns. But instead of placing the porch on the front of the house as was the style, he built it facing the sloping lawns that lead to the Potomac River below. Here, the Washingtons' endless parade of guests would sit on Windsor chairs, brought outdoors from the large hall in the evenings, hoping to catch a cool breeze from the river.

Irregular silhouettes, often featuring fanciful turrets and towers, were a signature of the Queen Anne style of Victorian architecture. Flamboyant porches were often incorporated into the facade. A rounded corner of a wraparound porch makes an out-of-traffic spot for table and chairs, or a porch swing.

In the seven decades of Queen Victoria's reign, L-shaped porches, wraparounds, arcaded loggias, attached gazebos, and asymmetrical placement of porches became commonplace. Timber cottages and stone castles were treated to light, curvilinear gingerbread trim or to massive detail. The "Painted Ladies" of San Francisco, the startling summer cottages of the Camp Grounds on Martha's Vineyard, the beach houses of Cape May, New Jersey, attest to the diversity and inventiveness of Victorian style.

The Victorians not only added porches to their domestic architectural vernacular, they glorified porches in the form of resort architecture. With a new and profound concern for healthful, outdoor living, nineteenth-century families made pilgrimages to the seashore and mountains in search of restorative fresh air. Vast resort hotels soon sprang up, all with expansive porches.

In 1890 the bungalow style appeared, its small, personal scale marking a breakthrough for middle-class housing. Now the focus was on how average families lived (versus the earlier focus on the homes of the well-to-do), and nearly every home boasted a front porch with a shingled railing.

Throughout the nineteenth century, porches remained a constant theme but with the advent of the twentieth, interest in porches began to wane. As the first decades of the new century passed, the porch came to be regarded as old-fashioned, and the desire for all things modern pushed porch living into decline.

Modernism—as expressed in the prairie style of Frank Lloyd Wright as well as Art Deco and other lean designs—ignored the porch, for the most part. And by the fifties, with the introduction of inexpensive tract housing, television, and air-conditioning, the focus shifted indoors and the porch all but disappeared from the home-building scene.

Many Victorian summer cottages—like this dainty, gingerbread-encrusted example—boasted an abundance of porch space, with outdoor "rooms" jutting out from upstairs bedrooms as well as surrounding the lower floor. The family would spend most of their time during the warm, humid summers out-of-doors, eating, conversing, and even sleeping on their versatile porches.

CHAPTER ONE

A Porch for Every Home

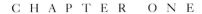

Above: The quirks and fancies of some Victorian architects produced whimsical houses with highly imaginative designs. Here, a variation on the Queen Anne theme—with its requisite turret and odd dormers—boasts a curious raised porch that wraps around the front, terminating on one end in a glassed-in section. To the rear sits a more informal screened-in area.

Left: Solitude, tranquillity, and peaceful isolation are the hallmarks of this massive porch, which overlooks the shores of a rocky cove. Unusually heavy brackets on supporting columns are reminiscent of the structural underpinnings of old whaling ships that plied the waters nearby a century or more ago.

For every type of house and for every family's style, there is a perfect porch. Whether you want a quiet outdoor niche where family members can lounge with a good summer read or a casual front porch that inspires passing neighbors to stop and chat, chances are that sometime in the past a porch style emerged that was designed to foster those very things.

Tall classical columns grace an elegant front porch in a setting where the living is easy. A long brick walk through immaculately kept gardens enhances the sense of graciousness and well-bred style, while the simple wicker rockers—one for Mama and two for the little ones—strike a cozy, comforting note. Here eager children may await visiting friends or relatives, or rest from a spirited game of croquet on the lawn.

The Front Porch

The front porch is a house's public face, the transitional space between street and home. It's where guests are greeted, strangers are assessed, families gather, and the comings and goings of the community are followed.

Calvert Vaux, an English-born architect who became a major influence in the development of American architecture, wrote in 1857 that "The veranda is perhaps the most specially American feature of a country house, and nothing can compensate for its absence."

Some front porches face neither the street nor the drive but a magnificent lakefront view. The deep recesses of this log home's front porch are large enough for entertaining yet intimate enough for quiet contemplation on misty mornings. Note the elegance of the Chippendalelike porch railing uniquely executed in rustic, rough-hewn wood.

Most of Vaux's hundreds of designs featured large front porches or verandas, which he discussed in his writing in great detail. In describing country residences, he wrote, "The porch or entrance suggests itself as having the priority of claim to our notice....This part of the design is the first that appeals to the attention of the visitor and admits of much character and expression."

Some architectural historians say that the front porch really came into its own after 1840, when leisure time became a part of people's lives due to industrialization and an increased labor force resulting from a large immigrant population. No less influential was the interest in healthful living. New information about the spread of disease encouraged exposure to fresh air, producing a trend toward outdoor activities.

Left: A group of rocking chairs is poised for visitors on the front porch of this beach town Victorian cottage. Vibrant blue trim accents repeat the blue of the vertical siding, which, along with the pointed-arch windows and door frame, are typical of Gothic Revival architecture. The porch railing, with its diamond-shaped inserts, is particularly appealing.

Opposite: Vertical siding, a cross-gable front, leaded windows, and intricate tracery detailing are all hallmarks of the Gothic Revival. The front porch of this circa 1844 gem is adorned with lacy, open woodwork on the support columns and along its fanciful roof. Note how the gothic design of the settee and chair on the porch are faultlessly matched to their domain.

Another holdover from the Victorian sense of the porch is the glimpse into the world of the family it bestows. A front porch says so much about the people who live there: on Front Street, High Street, and Main Street in small towns and villages everywhere, front porches are adorned with swings, flowerpots, flags, and striped awnings. Their owners dress them up with close attention to detail, displaying a charming pride of place. Front porches are places to show off, to offer a small public view of the way we live.

In New Orleans, the cast-iron railed, second-story porches were the ideal place to participate in the revelry of the Vieux Carre—from a respectable distance. The diminutive gingerbread porches of the crowded

The front porch of many an early house is little more than an oversized door hood supported by simple columns intended to shelter the front door from snow and rain when visitors come to call. The pair of heavy white-painted benches facing each other on either side of this modest porch may have been an afterthought rather than part of the original plan. Note how their positioning interferes ever so slightly with the short flight of stairs under the front door.

Camp Grounds at Oak Bluffs, Martha's Vineyard, rewarded their inhabitants with a bit of privacy as they enjoyed the close proximity of their like-minded neighbors.

The front porches of Charleston's downtown mansions, some raised up a half-story from the street, maintained an aloof nature, while the rustic front porches of Adirondack cabins and lodges beckoned visitors to swap recipes and tall tales.

Early Dutch Colonial houses featured a *stoep*, or stoop, under their flying gutter eaves. These stoops were essentially small front porches supported by pillars. Most were fitted with a pair of painted benches—many of them built into the porch structure—facing each other on either side of the front door.

In Florida's Key West, tiny cottages called conch houses are incomplete without a railed front porch to shade the long narrow house beyond. Conch house porches are often colorfully painted and swathed with hanging baskets of flowers.

The shape of front porches changed as the technology of the time grew. In cold winter areas, porches were kept shallow to allow the low winter sun to warm and illuminate interior spaces. But with central heating and electric light, porches could be deeper, making them shadier, more private places.

After World War I, front porches and grand, wraparound verandas lost favor—in part because of the advent of the automobile. People no longer sat on the veranda in their free time. They went for a ride. And the noise and fumes from traffic made sitting on the front porch less attractive. By this time, too, houses were being built closer together, and privacy became an issue. Smaller porches on the side or rear of the house soon became the norm. Today, though, a renaissance in porch architecture is occurring, and front porches are often included in the plans for newly constructed houses. In some new planned communities, front porches are mandated on every house in an effort to resurrect a small-town ambiance.

The wide, covered entrance of this back porch serves to frame lovely long-distance views across gardens and lawns to the sea. An interesting design particular is the rectangular, latticelike detail within the triangular pediment, which could be interpreted as a protective gate drawn up to allow one to pass through to the scene beyond.

The Back Porch

The back porch in days past was a personal place. Frequently of modest construction, this homely addition was a place for working, playing, storing goods, and perhaps sleeping.

It was here that the lady of the house left instructions for the milkman, ice was delivered, and the knife sharpener set up his tools. At farmhouses across the land, the back porch was where muddy boots would be deposited to await the next day's labor, where freshly picked vegetables would be husked and cleaned, and where the hired man would come for his wages.

Above: On a wide expanse of back porch, a pair of white-painted Adirondack chairs have been pulled out of the shadows into the sun. The clean lines and crisp look of this classic design affords a touch of simple elegance in any setting.

Right: A wonderful view isn't a prerequisite to good back porch design, but it does make porch sitting that much more pleasant. A sandy inlet offers a changing panorama of sail boats, bathers, and sea birds from the comforts of a wicker swing. Care must be taken in stormy weather to secure vulnerable porch furnishings, including hanging baskets of flowers.

The sweeping curve of this porch overlooking the water reminds one of the deck of an ocean liner—there is nothing but sky on the horizon. Cushioned deck chairs reinforce the notion of traveling in style. Note the formal styling of the wooden planters. The cube-shaped containers are known as "caisses Versailles," a style that originated at Versailles in the seventeenth century.

In grander homes, the back porch served as the servants' and tradesmen's entrance to the house; it was where laundry would be hung on stormy days and where the household help might sit for a few minutes after the day's work was done.

But until the advent of indoor plumbing, the back porch wasn't always the most pleasant place to spend time, particularly in the morning. Calvert Vaux, the nineteenth-century designer whose hundreds of affordable house plans were built throughout rural and suburban landscapes, included back porches in nearly every design. Yet in his extensive writings, he rarely mentions the back porch, perhaps because it was taken for granted or because its status was so low. He did write, "the kitchen veranda, facing south, provides a servant's entrance, and is convenient for hanging out clothes under cover in rainy weather." He also wrote, "an inclosure of the veranda supplies a space for a pantry and sink room." Back porches were simply utilitarian.

Wide-open vistas of farm fields and
meadows are framed by the posts of a
countrified back porch. Though hardly
rustic, the natural colors and relatively
unadorned design speak of a subtle
"home on the range" character.
Furnished here with a solitary rattan
chair, this large porch could happily
accommodate a larger gathering of furniture—perhaps a big plank table with
ladder-back chairs for a barbecue dinner or a collection of twig chairs and
tables arranged for comfortable conversation. The angular lines of the porch
will soften considerably as the
young vines trained on the railing
spread further.

The crisp white columns of this round porch repeat the forms of birch trees in the surrounding landscape. A graceful and serene structure, this porch seems to float in its space. The simple set of white wicker is unobtrusive and allows the architectural design to dominate. Another approach to furnishing this unusual porch might include vintage deck chairs with awning-striped cushions, over-sized natural wicker with cabbage rose chintz upholstery, or a sleek Art Deco-inspired metal chaise with matching side chairs and a massive coffee table. The point is, a porch this beautiful sets a faultless stage for nearly any style of furnishing.

With the growth of suburban communities, families directed their leisure time to the backyard, and patios and decks became the transitional space between indoors and out, while mud rooms, laundry rooms, and garages replaced the back porch as a work space.

Thirty years later, the porch is making a comeback as home owners rediscover the attractive and comfortable space it affords. But this time around, the back porch is not a place for homey industry. It has become the new family center—a warm-weather spot for togetherness, entertaining, relaxing, and dining.

Because it is covered, a porch can be used in even the heaviest rainstorm, furniture is not exposed as harshly to the elements, and even more importantly, our skin can be saved from the dangers of over-exposure to the sun's damaging rays.

Suburban dwellers are adding large porches to the backs of their houses where decks might have been placed only a few years ago. Frequently, these porches extend from one side of the house to the other, often opening onto the kitchen and family, dining, and living rooms, making the porch an extension of nearly every public space in the home.

Though we often think of porches in the context of Victorian and country styling, a contemporary home can also be enhanced by a porch. The architect who designed this back porch has taken a modern approach to a Greek Revival theme. Built almost like a small out-building, this clapboard structure has a pedimented roof with clever half-circle cutouts. The half-walls add to its air of solidity but the windowlike openings give the porch an airy, breezy flair.

The Side Porch

Right: The side porch, approached here by a path through the garden, is typical of the bracketed Italian Villa style, where odd angles, multiple rooflines, and asymmetry dominated the design scheme. As is the case of the porch pictured here, many side porches are simply a part of a larger porch that wraps around two or more sides of a house. A door to the interior and a separate roofline define the distinction between side, front, or rear with greater clarity. When especially large houses are divided into several apartments, side doors with an accompanying porch can make the transition from single-family home to multiple dwelling more comfortable from an aesthetic point of view, and offer residents a relatively private out-of-doors space.

Opposite: In new construction, side porches are experiencing a resurgence in popularity. Often situated near the family room, the side porch—with its equal access to side yard and indoor play space—becomes a favorite of children, who can take over the area without fear of being underfoot or ruining the decor of front porch and parlor.

If the front porch is like the welcoming smile of a home, the side porch might be considered a bit more reticent. It's tucked away out of the limelight—a little more private, even intimate. What better place than the shady side porch for the quiet retreat of a hammock or a deeply cushioned wicker chair.

Side porches are often simply a continuation of a large front porch that wraps around the facade of a house. Sometimes, though, side porches are designed to stand on their own.

The Italian Villa style, popular around the time of the Civil War, featured small side porches placed in odd corners and out-of-the-way niches. Tiny balconies and second-, third-, or fourth-story porches, complete with

Around the turn of the century, the quest for healthy living reached staggering proportions, resulting in a trend toward sleeping porches. The healthful benefits of fresh air were extolled by experts and this advice was taken to heart throughout the country. Sitting out in the fresh air on the porch, which had always been a pleasurable pursuit, now carried the added importance of being good for a body. It wasn't a long stretch from sitting on the porch to sleeping on the porch.

Soon, second-story porches were sprouting on the sides or backs of houses everywhere. Sunrooms and porches on the ground level were topped by sleeping porches in order to accommodate the new concept. Some were screened or even glassed in while others were left en pleine aire. *The second story was generally favored for sleeping porches, in part because the air was thought to be better at higher elevations, but also because the porch's height afforded some privacy from the street.*

rich ornamental detail, were used as sleeping porches or for the quiet escape they provided. Awnings, shades, latticework, and plants added to the sense of privacy.

Other Victorian architectural styles, particularly the later Shingle, Eastlake, and Stick styles, incorporated side porches or verandas into their designs, especially when a seaside or mountain view could be seen from its position.

Wraparound Porches

When we think of a veranda, the image of a wide, wraparound porch comes immediately to mind. These sweeping porches are as functional as they are decorative. A broad expanse of porch was originally designed to keep interior spaces cool in the summer, protect exterior walls from the elements, and provide a covered outdoor space where breezes could be enjoyed. The first wraparound porches were found in tropical or desert communities, where they provided an essential shield from the harsh sun and heat. Adobe haciendas in the Southwest were often simple squares with a wide porch built around three or four sides of the house. Inside, a covered porch encircled an open courtyard and served as the linking corridor to interior rooms. The broad verandas that wrapped around plantation houses in the South were called galleries. They were often raised up a level to keep the living quarters dry and served as exterior hallways, much like hacienda-style courtyard porches.

By the middle of the Victorian era, porches that formed an L- or U-shape around the front and sides of the house were seen in towns all over the country. Due to the irregular silhouette of Queen Anne, Shingle, and Stick style homes, the Victorians favored porches that jutted out into octagonal, square, or semicircular appendages topped by a shingled turret. Often these turrets were decorated with a metal finial at one or more corners. Some were adorned with benches built into the angles of the space. These porches lend themselves especially well to entertaining and are a joy to decorate with vintage wicker and lush plants.

New homes are only rarely built with wraparound front porches, but many families are opting to add large back porches that wrap partway around one of the sides of the house. Usually these side spaces are accessible from the kitchen, or dining, living, or family rooms, making them ideal areas for entertaining.

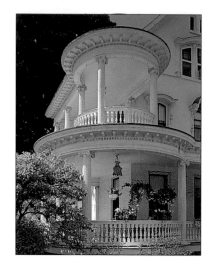

Above : Resembling an intricately constructed wedding cake, this exquisite two-tiered wraparound porch is an endearing example of how far Victorian architecture carried whimsy and exaggerated ornamentation. Note the unifying use of brackets, which surround both of the rounded porch projections and continue along the entire length of the cornices.

Right: An eclectic and much-loved collection of vintage wicker graces the multisided end of a large wraparound porch made distinctive by its especially attractive railing. The wrought-iron plant hooks attached to the columns await warmer weather, when they'll be graced by large wire baskets overflowing with colorful annuals.

An irregular silhouette, pointed turrets, complicated rooflines, and riotous combinations of surface materials are all hallmarks of the Queen Anne style, which was introduced by British architects during the Philadelphia Centennial Exposition in 1876. Wraparound porches provided yet more opportunities for an abundance of ornamentation; such decorative possibilities include the frieze of flowers that runs around the paneled fascia board of the octagonal porch end pictured here. The floral theme is repeated under the second floor roof. The same motif can be seen under the roof of the dormer end, near another small porch, this one perhaps once designated for sleeping.

Summertime pleasures are obviously the order of the day for the owners of this country house. A ceiling fan, thick-cushioned rattan sofa, and rocker attest to the importance given to creature comforts here. The generous proportions of this screened porch make it highly adaptable to a broad range of family activities.

Screened - In Porches

At the height of black fly season, in warm wet climes where the mosquitoes are the size of bumblebees, and at the shore when the horseflies are on the warpath, there is no porch as useful as a screened-in one. Before the advent of inexpensive, factory-made metal screening in the 1880s, people used wooden blinds and louvered shutters to keep insects off the porch.

Sometimes upper-story porches were screened in to provide a warm-weather sleeping space, or small side porches were fitted with screens to provide insect-free dining or lounging places. Overall, though, screened porches were more likely to be found on weekend cottages at the shore or in the mountains

This screened porch evokes a slightly formal mood. Instead of a delightful assortment of heirlooms, fleamarket finds, and quaint collectibles, there is a matching set of vintage wicker, including two tables and a pretty lamp. The sky blue ceiling, dark blue stripes of the chair cushions, and jar of posies prevent the decor from appearing severe.

and on the porches of modest bungalows and farmhouses in the country than on the grand homes of city and town folk. Yet a screened porch is a wonderfully comfortable place to be. The breeze can easily penetrate the fine mesh of the screens, which also reduce the strength of penetrating sunlight.

Screened porches are a selling point in today's real estate market because they are so conducive to family life. Children can play safely on a screened porch but still have the benefits of being outdoors, and dining is pleasant when insects are kept at bay. If you are planning to screen in an existing porch and your home has some significant historic merit, you may want to check with your local zoning officer to find out about building codes, as screens can detract from a building's historical integrity. However, removable screens may be a workable solution for your situation and can generally be added with few structural alterations.

Glassed-In Porches

As porches fell out of favor, those that weren't pulled off were often closed in with solid walls. A more aesthetic approach was to enclose the porch with windows, creating what was soon dubbed the sunroom. Often sunrooms weren't heated but, like greenhouses, collected enough warmth from the sun to be comfortable even on winter days. The room simply wouldn't be used at night during cold weather. To

extend a sunroom's useful hours, it could be opened onto the rest of the house with French doors or a wide entryway.

Many glassed-in porches are two-story affairs, pairing the sunroom with an open-air or screened-in porch either above the sunroom or below it, on the ground level. Second-story glassed-in porches were frequently used as sleeping porches, while those on the ground level often became extensions of living or dining rooms.

Opposite: This glassed-in porch has the luxurious feeling of a greenhouse, thanks to the addition of wide panels of glass that serve as a roof. New insulating windows will help keep this porch cool in summer and warm in winter, relatively speaking. In such a space, your sun-loving plants are guaranteed to flourish.

Left: If solar panels or a heating system is installed, a glassed-in porch can become a year-round retreat—witness the thick blanket of snow carpeting the landscape outside this classic sunroom. The beautiful arched design of the windows gives this porch an elegant appeal, and the curve is subtly mirrored in the graceful back of the settee. A sisal rug warms the slate floor while preserving the natural look that has been carefully cultivated with rattan furniture, upholstery in earth tones, and plenty of potted plants.

Opposite: Conservatories were a favorite of the Victorians and continue to enthrall us today. Their airy design and versatility have made them a cherished, if somewhat less usual, addition to homes all across the country. The shelf running at seat level in this charming example provides an ideal resting spot for a selection of flowering plants and an ornamental birdcage. Cast-metal furniture is the perfect match, both historically and decoratively, for this spacious conservatory.

Left: Home owners looking for rooms that adapt to their needs will often design a porch with removable screens and windows in order to have year-round, or nearly so, use. Porches like the one pictured here might be fitted with glass or even clear plastic panels during the cooler months. Once warm weather arrives, screen panels replace the glass.

Opposite: Few rooms are more inviting than a well-furnished sunroom, especially on bright, cool days when the sun is high enough to share its warmth. In the sunroom pictured here, all the elements of success have been incorporated. The windows are oversized and designed to open so that breezes will circulate well on very warm days. Wicker is used exclusively in the furnishings, including a magazine basket and a small coffee table that also serves as a storage basket, giving the decor a unified look. Lush, healthy plants, vintage lighting fixtures, and a clutter of throw pillows make effective accents without feeling too busy.

Right: Dark green reproduction wicker, with its cabbage rose chintz cushions, is especially attractive when combined with the warm, natural wood of floors, railings, and columns on a lofty raised porch. Depending on the season, screens or glass are the only things that separate guests from the great outdoors, making this an ideal summer retreat for reading or an afternoon chat over tall glasses of iced tea.

CHAPTER TWO

The Beauty of Porch Living

Above: Massive classical columns and a simple, sturdy railing bespeak a substantial house where life is good, and guests are graciously received. Though set for a solitary libation, this antique table would surely welcome an additional glass.

Left: It's not difficult to decipher that this expansive Victorian porch is the scene of frequent and bustling activity. A wicker desk might serve as a homework center in the late afternoon after having been the site of intensive party planning earlier in the day. The round table, so attractively draped in chintz and surrounded by an unmatched collection of robin's egg blue wicker chairs, is set for coffee but is equally adept at breakfast, lunch, dinner, or bridge.

It's a part-time room. A home to plants. It's where you go to meditate or do stretching exercises. On the porch, casual family meals are enjoyed alfresco and elegant parties demonstrate your entertaining skill. Porches are much more than a preface to the home's interior, and here we'll explore the many ways your porch can acquire a personality that fits your needs perfectly.

An upper-story porch, perhaps just off a bedroom, becomes an out-of-doors sitting room—a quiet, personal place where cares and responsibilities might be put aside, at least for a moment. When the porch possesses an extraordinary view, as does the one pictured here, it becomes even easier to unwind and recharge. Though a view isn't essential, a comfortable chair and a sense of being far away are. If the porch is situated too near busy neighbors, decorative screens, a vine-covered trellis, an awning, or even billowing curtains made of mosquito netting might be used to create the sense of privacy and remoteness that allows even the most tightly wound workaholic to find refuge.

Finding Respite and Solitude

In days gone by, porches were necessary, functional parts of the architecture of houses. Built to keep parlors and bedrooms cool, to provide a comfortable place to sleep in summer, or as a service entry at the back of the house, porches fulfilled a need.

Today, people are building or restoring porches to fulfill a very modern need: the need for relaxation. The porch has become a place to unwind, offering an opportunity to be outdoors and listen to the sounds of nature after a day spent at work in central air-conditioning. It's restorative and calming to be

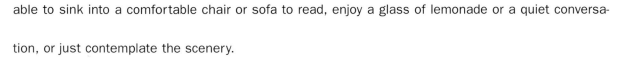

Above: Paying attention to the little details is one of the ways we can assure ourselves a sense of well-being. Instead of gulping breakfast on the run, the owner of this porch has taken a few extra minutes to pour a glass of juice and to read the paper before diving into the day. Early in the morning the porch may be just the place to treat yourself to a little solitude and relaxation.

Above left: The elements that make a porch a place for rest and repose include a chair (or two or three if you enjoy the company of others), a table to hold a drink or snack, and perhaps a cozy quilt to wrap around yourself on cool misty mornings.

able to sink into a comfortable chair or sofa to read, enjoy a glass of lemonade or a quiet conversation, or just contemplate the scenery.

If you're going to be using your porch as a private place to unwind after work, plants and flowers will help refresh a beleaguered spirit, and if you choose the right varieties you can add the wonderful benefit of fragrance (see Chapter Five). Outfit your porch with only the most comfortable chairs and sofas, the kind you can easily sink into. Banish all straight-back chairs or smallish settees and opt instead for a sofa you can stretch out on completely. Consider chaise lounges and chairs with matching ottomans so you can put your feet up whenever you sit. And remember that rocking chairs, porch swings, and hammocks are all well-loved for the peaceful feelings they bring.

Morning easily flows into afternoon and on into the evening without one feeling the slightest inclination to leave this exquisite porch—unless it's to make a quick foray into the kitchen to prepare meals. Of course, the view of the water is mesmerizing. The well-placed bistro table and chairs permit lazy relaxation to continue through meals, after which it's time to return to the thick, inviting cushions of the sleep-inducing wicker chaise.

The Beauty of Porch Living

Opposite: Dappled sunlight accents the shadows of nearby trees on the polished floor of this peaceful porch, which has the feel of a comfortable family room. A cat has claimed a snug spot on a brightly cushioned rattan sofa whose colors are repeated in big pots of flowers. An abundance of plants, books, magazines, and well-loved objects, along with the presence of an affectionate pet, are often elements that contribute to relaxed porch living.

Left: A stark, uncluttered approach—where the stillness of the scenery takes the porch sitter outside of himself or herself—is found in this serene space. Here, a collection of rocking chairs stands ready to accommodate guests, with nothing more than a book or two to distract them from the view.

Make sure to select fabrics that don't require a lot of care and designate a large basket for newspapers, magazines, books, and other reading material so that you don't have to waste time searching around the house for an article you began reading last night. Writing materials, vases of flowers, scented candles, and a butler's tray or a large coffee table for drinks are all small touches that will help set a quiet, tranquil mood. A spare, clean decor with minimal furnishings and reduced clutter provides a sense of calm. Smooth woods and cool, monochromatic color schemes are considered restive, while a single, exotic orchid or a piece of art—a sculpture, wood carving, or painting with a mysterious quality—can provide the meditative atmosphere that is an antidote for stress.

Alfresco Dining

A‍bove: Pots of lilies, tulips, and other blooms seem to merge garden, terrace, and porch. A small café table surrounded by decorative iron chairs is set in the center of this floral stage, and is ideal for meals taken out-of-doors. The generous proportions of the space offer nearly unlimited options for dining, whether *en famille* or with dozens of guests.

O‍pposite: The graceful, arched bays of this porch are echoed in shadows on the wall. Here is a spot where an experienced hostess has perfected the formula for successful alfresco meals. It's helpful when the kitchen is not too far off, especially when hot foods are on the menu. Electric hot-trays or chafing dishes heated with candles or tins of paraffin are useful too.

Though the pleasures of a solitary afternoon spent lazing on the porch are immeasurable, wonderful summertime memories weave a beautiful life tapestry when you share a meal out on the porch. Reserve some time during the summer season for a Sunday morning brunch with your family. Or make your meal a candlelit dinner for two while the children are away at camp. Summer's slow pace is perfect for casual gatherings, so be sure to mark a few Saturday nights on the calendar for cocktails and hors d'oeuvres or a leisurely potluck supper with friends.

Dining alfresco doesn't have to be complicated. If your porch furniture doesn't yet include a table for dining, find a sturdy card table and cover it with white linen, a summer quilt, or a colorful, billowy sheet. Or carry the old picnic table up from the yard and top it with a gingham cloth.

Fill a vase or mason jar with snapdragons, cosmos, or zinnia blooms from your garden and place two or three votive candles in the center of the table, and you have the beginnings of a lovely dinner, whether for family or friends. Use hurricane or kerosene lamps in the background on end tables or hang them on the wall to give the evening a glow. Add wind chimes for background music. Weights sewn in or tacked on around the hem of your tablecloth will prevent a wayward breeze from lifting it up.

And do bring out all your prettiest things. Linens, china, Wedgwood platters, and fine silver add to the ambience of a romantic tête-à-tête and make for a more special, convivial atmosphere when serving dinner for friends and family. Whimsical flea market finds are fun to use on the porch—fifties-style creamers and sugar bowls, Fiestaware, vintage serving trays, French bistro plates, and Depression glass goblets are all delightful conversation starters.

Outdoor meals are one of the true joys of summer but they are too often ruined by marauding insects. If your porch is unscreened, give some thought to the ways you can prevent buggy pests from invading. Consider tenting the table area with fine mosquito netting. Not only is this a practical solution for ridding your repast of flying insects, it imparts an exotic quality to the setting. If your dining space is too large for this option to be realistic, you can purchase small, screened domes that can be set over dishes to keep them free of flies. Citronella candles, too, are a favorite way of clearing the air of mosquitoes, and their flickering light is a pleasure as well.

Colorful plastic dinnerware, available through many specialty housewares shops and department stores, can be used for salads, desserts, or the main course, especially if children are among your dinner companions. Use cloth napkins since they don't blow away as easily as paper ones, and if you do choose paper plates, place them in bamboo liners so they won't leak or fly across the table with a gust of wind. Mix and match colors and styles for a sense of fun and put the focus of the meal on friendship rather than on the place settings.

Keep tray-shaped baskets handy for carrying cutlery, napkins, condiments, and other essentials to the table. Pitchers of iced tea and lemonade on a butler's tray, tea cart, or side table, along with an ice bucket and glasses, will prevent needless to and fro from the kitchen.

Opposite: The fresh tastes of summer are never enjoyed more than when they are consumed out-of-doors. The set table on the porch of this country farmhouse is inviting in its simplicity.

Left: Amusing and personal decorative objects, including vintage China dolls, a long-necked heron, and a brass birdcage, become the main course—at least visually—in the corner of a narrow porch set up for a midsummer meal. Tasseled shades keep the sun from penetrating too far into the shadows. The low-hanging birdcage, the tall sculpture, and the potted standard tree all serve to draw the eye away from the very high porch ceiling that might otherwise diminish the vignette's feeling of intimacy.

Extra chairs can be found at tag sales and there's no need to worry about finding matching sets. Mismatched chairs will add interest to the scheme. Even in formal dining rooms, decorators now routinely mix up different styles of chairs and achieve wonderful effects. And since the porch bespeaks a laid-back lifestyle, you have endless options. If you prefer a slightly more pulled-together look, paint chairs of different styles and vintages all the same color. The common hue will unify the scheme despite the chairs' varying characters. If storage for extra chairs poses a dilemma, consider buying a few folding chairs and outfitting them with dressy padded slipcovers, which you can sew for yourself or purchase ready-made. Scrap the rules and concentrate on making your dining festive. Feel free to be creative with seating and accessories, letting thoughts of your guests' comfort be your only guide.

Entertaining

Because the porch is an extension of our living space, we enjoy dining, playing, and relaxing there. And of course, when we entertain, the porch—whether it's a grand, sweeping veranda or a cozy screened-in affair—can provide additional space for guests.

Ladies' lunches, bridge games, cocktail hours, and children's birthday parties all take on a special flair when you site them on the porch. If you are planning a bridal or baby shower for a friend or relative, think about having it on the porch rather than in your living room or a rented space. Dress the porch the same way you would any other party spot; the outdoor location automatically adds a breezy, relaxed quality to the event.

At holiday time, invite friends to join you in caroling in your neighborhood, then serve hot chocolate and cookies on the porch. Everyone will be bundled up and you can keep the cocoa hot in thermoses.

On a rainy weekend, when your children are complaining about having nothing to do, help them organize a porch party with their friends. Bring out the CD player, plan games, and serve simple finger foods, and they'll soon forget what boredom means.

When planning a big party, don't forget to include the porch in your thinking. Situate your bar at one end of the porch and set trays of hors d'oeuvres on side tables throughout the room. If you are working with a caterer, discuss in advance the flow of food and beverages from kitchen to porch.

To create a truly festive atmosphere, use as many candles or votive lights as you have tabletops for—nothing sets a mood better than candlelight. Fill vases with fresh flowers and gather all your potted plants from around the house. Consider timing your party to coincide with the blooming of wisteria,

Above: Don't wait to use your porch for entertaining til you have the time and inclination to plan a formal dinner with all the trimmings—invite friends to an impromtu wine and cheese party. Every event becomes a memorable affair when you choose a setting as refined as this classic porch.

Opposite: Every warm-weather holiday makes a perfect excuse for a party on the porch. Bring out your best—including beautiful dishware, cloth napkins and place mats, and imaginative table decorations— to create an occasion that is truly something to remember.

roses, lilacs, or lilies—the delicate fragrance of the blossoms will waft over your guests in a gentle ode to summer.

Nearly any party you would plan for inside your house can be arranged for the porch as well. The only restricting factors are space and temperature. Of course, if your porch is in plain sight or within hearing range of your neighbors, you'll want to make an effort to keep the noise level down—or plan on inviting them too!

Opposite: Invitations to a luncheon or brunch in this sunroom are highly prized. And no wonder; a charmingly set table and attention to the smallest detail have here been elevated to the status of an art. Note the lovely vintage table linens and the use of several different patterns of china.

Left: Meals for weekend guests become help-yourself affairs when a wicker table is piled high with delicious fresh food. Guests who rise with the sun might enjoy coffee and a light breakfast before their hosts are ready to face the day. Prepare the coffeepot and place muffins and breakfast breads in sealed containers on a table on the porch. Leave a note about where to find milk and butter and encourage guests to enjoy the tranquillity of an early morning spent on the porch.

CHAPTER THREE

Furnishing
with Style

Close your eyes and think of a porch from your past. You might

picture a contented family sitting in slat-backed rockers or deeply

cushioned wicker chairs. Perhaps there's an antique, marble-

topped, wrought-iron table littered with magazines. You might

even conjure up a memory of a shaded sleeping porch with a

creaky daybed covered with colorful, handmade quilts.

Above: This porch has been
designed less for leisure than for
activity—horticultural activity, to be
precise. But a sturdy chair provides
a place for a few moments of rest
when the need arises.

Left: Book group meetings, a get-
together of the hospital benefit planning committee, lunch with the kids, or
just a nice sit-down alone...no matter
the activity, all are done in style and
comfort on this exquisitely furnished
porch. Shiny black cast-iron benches,
antique tables, and prized objets d'art
set an elegant, refined tone. Note how
well the black arched trim on the sisal
rug defines the space and seems to
repeat the design of the iron benches.

Chairs, Rockers, and Settees

The sleek lines of a teak deck chair recall the days of leisurely transatlantic cruises and grand world tours. While vintage versions of thèse timeless chairs still exist, manufacturers recognize good design when they see it and have begun making reproductions. These newly produced versions are available in various woods and colors, and many come with cushions. A deck chair like the one pictured above will work in nearly any design scheme from contemporary to Victorian to colonial. Add custom-made cushions—perhaps in pinstripes, bold solid colors, or oversized prints—for comfort. Provide a chenille throw for warmth and a small side table to hold drinks and a book for consummate porch pleasure.

An essential element in the decor of your porch, seating in all its styles and variations should enhance the overall design, be compatible with your lifestyle, and, of course, be practical. Above all, a comfortable, well-placed rocking chair or settee is an invitation to relax.

In order to select the most appropriate seating for your porch, ask yourself a few questions. What purpose will chairs, rockers, and settees serve on the porch? Is creature comfort the number one requirement or does gracious entertaining in elegant surroundings more aptly describe your porch's use? Do you need seating that will withstand the exuberance of young children and not-quite-trained pets? Perhaps your furniture will need to adapt to many different uses.

You'll also want to think about practical matters. Selection of fabric and materials for furniture must depend in part on how much shelter from rain and strong sun the furniture will have. If you don't have extra space for winter storage, you'll have to choose furniture that will stand up to harsh weather. Space is also a consideration: if a large settee would crowd the room, opt for a smaller piece. Measure the heights of furniture as well as that of windows and railings; otherwise you might be faced with a sofa back that obstructs the view from the window. Also think about whether the chairs will remain in place or whether you'll want to move them around for dining, card-playing, or conversation.

A set of wicker—a settee with matching chair and rocker—is the quintessential porch furnishing. Whether it's a new, weather-resistant set or a vintage piece from the 1920s, wicker just looks and feels

The actual elements of porch furnishings are relatively simple—chairs, tables, settees. It is the selection of just the right chair or table and the decorative accessories and objects that sets the tone and style of the porch. This porch is simply furnished but the effect is not entirely austere—note the delicate curlicues on the wicker rocker and whimsical wicker elephant table. Imagine how different the same porch would appear if it were furnished more extravagantly. What kind of visual effect would a pair of steamer chairs have if they replaced the rocker? Or picture this porch with the addition of a rug, hanging planters of colorful annuals, or an étagère displaying a collection of folk art or vintage pottery. If you think of your porch as a blank palette and the furnishings as the paint, you will be on the right track.

A creative blend of furniture styles in this long, narrow sunroom turns a relatively plain space into an interesting office, sitting room, or out-of-the-way retreat. Since this porch is not open to the elements, there is ample opportunity for displaying decorative details, including paintings, an antique upholstered three-legged stool, and small, fragile collectibles. Built-in shades, some of which slide from the bottom up, lend privacy, perhaps for overnight guests who will sleep on futon pillows. At the far end of the porch, a narrow table that holds framed photos, paintings, and ceramic pieces might double as a desk, with plenty of room for a laptop computer and a phone.

like a lazy day on the porch. North American wicker, made from the mid-1850s on, was made of imported rattan, reeds, willow, cane, and man-made fibers.

Wicker furniture ranged dramatically from simple to wildly ornate, and many styles adopted the names of the resort towns where they were popular. Open basketry designs with squared chair backs came to be known as Bar Harbor style; wicker pieces with heart-shaped backs were considered to be in the Newport style; curved-back examples were called Southampton style; and Cape Cod wicker featured very tightly woven reeds. These basic styles have persevered—with a few variations—and are still made today.

There is no such thing as too much wicker, especially when it bedecks a large Victorian porch. The owner of this porch has lovingly assembled a delightful collection of vintage wicker in a number of styles. The square-lined Bar Harbor-styled wicker swing, suspended from the high ceiling from chains, looks great piled high with pillows and draped with an old quilt. The high-backed winged rocker is notable for its side pockets—the perfect place to stash magazines or a knitting project. And a diminutive child's rocker can always be counted on to add charm to porch decor. The collection of furniture includes a coffee table, footstool, side table, and lamp and plant stands, and although the styles are varied, they are subtly coordinated by the repeated use of two or three fabrics on pillows and upholstery.

In 1921, the Lloyd Manufacturing Company of Menominee, Michigan, invented a machine called the Lloyd loom that wove wicker furniture from a man-made fiber, and by 1930 about 85 percent of all American-made wicker was made from that fiber.

Gustav Stickley, a furniture maker whose angular, compact furniture designs launched the Craftsman and later the Mission styles, worked in wicker as well as oak. His designs, a reaction to the excesses of Victorian ornamentation and to the loss of quality workmanship that was a result of mass production, added yet another direction to both interior and porch decor.

Sometimes less is more. The refined, flowing, unadorned lines of the black metal settee pictured here couldn't be more appropriate or elegant. It looks as if it were designed specifically for this space, a recessed niche of a white lattice-walled porch. Or perhaps the porch was designed to hold the settee! Though usually less comfortable than a wicker settee with deep cushions or a slanted-seat Adirondack chair, cast- and wrought-iron furniture have a grace and distinction that is undeniable. Antique pieces are increasingly hard to come by, but many manufacturers and individual craftsmen are creating new pieces, which are available through catalogs, at craft shows, and from dealers. Iron furniture needs a fair amount of care, but furniture made from cast aluminum is relatively maintenance-free.

Later wicker manufacturers responded to changes in decorating taste, making the transition to French-inspired Art Deco and art moderne interests by designing gracefully curved rattan chairs and settees.

The Victorians and their successors into the 1920s and 1930s liked to use wicker in every room of the house, but its popularity began on the porch. Whatever the pattern or style, wicker chairs, rockers, and settees beckon you to come and "set a spell."

Vintage wicker, especially the Bar Harbor and Southampton styles, can be found at estate sales, flea markets, and antique shops, and the more elaborate antique pieces are available through dealers who specialize in wicker. New wicker is available in a variety of modern styles and is also being manufactured in reproduction styles, with some very inexpensive examples imported from China, the Philippines, Haiti, and Italy.

A few companies continue to make handcrafted wicker furniture in traditional designs while others produce sturdy, attractive machine-made wicker furniture—some from old designs, others updated for more contemporary tastes—that stand up to the weather and active family life.

Cast-iron furniture, once the stately queen of nineteenth-century garden furnishings, now takes pride of place on Victorian-style porches. Descendants of eighteenth-century hand-wrought metal furniture, the antiques we see today generally date from the mid-1800s to the beginning of the twentieth century. These mass-produced, cast-iron pieces originally graced the lavish gardens of the newly well-to-do.

Conforming to the tastes of the time, designs grew increasingly ornate and fanciful. Grape clusters, vines, acanthus leaves, honeysuckle, lilies, ferns, twigs, and other botanical motifs were immensely

popular, and were considered especially appropriate because they extended the garden theme. Decorative fretwork, laureling, nulling, fans, medallions, and cartouches were also incorporated into the backs, sides, and legs of chairs and settees. Seats were most often made in geometric, woven, slat, or grid patterns to provide some degree of comfort.

Patterns with pointed arches and quatrefoils catered to the intense interest in the Gothic Revival architectural style of the 1840s and 1850s. Looping curves of iron distinguish some Gothic-style benches and settees, as well.

Today, antique cast-iron furniture usually commands high prices at estate sales and from antiques dealers who specialize in garden furnishings. However, wonderful reproductions, many made from the original molds, are now available in both cast iron and aluminum. Many people prefer the weight and stature of cast iron, although it tends to be expensive and does require regular painting if it is exposed to the weather. Aluminum furniture is relatively maintenance-free and generally lower in price. Its light weight can be eminently practical if you'll need to move pieces around a lot.

Cast-metal furniture is most often painted black, white, or dark green. Intricate pieces with lots of deeply defined details can look especially attractive with a verdigris finish, which gives the piece the color of weathered antique bronze. Verdigris is a blue-green copper acetate used as a paint pigment.

Opposite: Stately columns support a classically styled porch with peaceful lakeside views. Here resides a traditional style of metal furniture that features low-slung backs and gracefully curved arms. The chairs are embellished with basket-weave backs surrounded by garlands, and have simple square cushions. The table, a simple glass-topped square, is part of the set.

Above left: A tiny niche in the wall under the porch roof becomes the defining space for an alfresco work area. Telephone time is spent in outdoor luxury, surrounded by sumptuous plantings and striking architectural elements. The metal and glass desk, though small, has room for the phone, a Rolodex file, some flowers, and a refreshing glass of orange juice. A complementary metal chair is softened with a thick green cushion.

By 1825 the rocking chair—an invention attributed by some to Benjamin Franklin—had become an institution. Rocking in a chair was thought to aid digestion, was recommended for invalids, and was considered essential for nursing mothers. At least one rocking chair could be found on nearly every porch, from the simplest cottage to the grandest country house. According to James Frewin, an English builder who visited the United States in 1938, "It is considered a compliment to give the stranger the rocking chair as a seat, and when there is more than one in the house, the stranger is always presented with the best."

Look for do-it-yourself kits in paint and art supply stores or ask your furniture dealer to suggest a professional painter who specializes in faux finishes.

Wrought-iron chairs and settees—in antique, reproduction, and contemporary designs—are often more angular than cast-iron pieces and usually feature curvilinear designs or patterns that resemble latticework. Contemporary pieces and reproductions are now being made in heavy-gauge steel. Older pieces will need maintenance if they are exposed to moisture, but newly manufactured steel furniture is made to be weather-resistant.

Wire furniture offers a lighter, airier look than its cast- or wrought-metal cousins. Debuting during the Victorian era, wire chairs and settees were constructed of intricately bent, curved, twisted, and scrolled strands of metal. Seats often resembled basketry while backs and legs were highly decorative flights of fancy.

In the last ten years, there has been a resurgence of interest in wire chairs and settees, and many reproductions of the original French garden furniture—most of them made in England—are now on the market. Wire furniture is usually painted white, which emphasizes its airy nature.

Metal chairs and settees are at home on an elaborate Victorian porch, but they also make a bold focal point within the clean lines of a contemporary structure. Because of their highly embellished nature, wire and cast-metal seating might seem out of place in a rustic setting, where other seating choices might make more design sense.

If iron seating is your choice for the porch, keep in mind that it is heavier to move than wicker, wood, or canvas chairs and settees. You'll want to give it a permanent spot on the porch to avoid scratching or marring the floor or, worse, dropping it on a bare toe! And remember, cast-iron and wire furniture hardly make a comfy seat to flop down in after work. Nor is it the spot you will choose for the times you want to curl up with a book.

A simple rocking chair is at home on any porch. Rockers lined up along a porch impart a classic country look, and no log cabin or Adirondack camp porch is complete without a rocker for watching the sun set, catching a breeze, or whiling away a lazy summer afternoon.

This matching chair and settee are reproductions of perennially popular twig styles. Outfitted with plump cushions and a pillow made from a discarded blue-checked tablecloth, these pieces make comfortable additions to this casual porch.

Right: Dark, rough-hewn beams, aging floor planks, and mottled stone combine with the different colors, textures, and styles of chairs, tables, and benches to present authentic country appeal. Squashes and drying herbs provide seasonal decor.

Opposite: The frame of this unusual rocker has been only partially finished, so that the knots, bumps, and other irregularities of the wood are clearly visible. This natural style is a perfect complement to the stained adobe walls and split-rail styling of this narrow gallery.

Rockers can have arms—or not. Rocking chairs—and side chairs for that matter—might have bar, arrow, lathe, ladder, or spindle backs, with seats made of rush, planks, splint, tape, or upholstery. They can be made using snowshoes or old cradle rockers, as in days long past, or they can emulate the bentwood Thonet-style rocker so popular in the 1960s. With such incredible variety of material and style, you're certain to find one that suits your porch—just be sure to have at least one!

For a rustic ambience, twig chairs and settees are a delightful choice. These rough-hewn designs, in yew, apple, and pear woods, originated in the eighteenth century as a snub to the pervasive formality of French styles. The romantic ideas of the early 1800s inspired a revival of twig and willow designs, which flourished throughout the nineteenth century. And with the Victorian Revival of the past fifteen years or so we've witnessed a renaissance of these graceful, naturalistic pieces.

When you search for furniture, set your priorities. Choose only things you really love and don't settle for something that's almost right. Hold out until you find exactly what you're looking for. And don't let yourself be limited by conventions set by others. There are no rules when it comes to your own taste.

Above: The emphasis on shape and color is the backbone of this simple setting. The gently rounded back of a twig rocker is repeated in the stone arches and oval wall piece. The dark, rough bark of the chair contrasts beautifully with smooth, pale walls.

Right: A quiet glassed-in porch, comfortably fitted with old-fashioned wicker, is perfect for reading or conversation. The traditional furniture is enlivened by a fanciful trompe l'oeil that turns a wall into an extension of the outdoors. A crisp, striped awning with scalloped edges imbues the room with a tentlike atmosphere.

U p h o l s t e r y

In years past, upholstery wasn't of major concern when purchasing chairs, rockers, and sofas for the porch. If upholstery was used outdoors at all, it was in the form of a small, thin cushion placed on the seat of a wicker chair; the cushion was covered in a durable cotton and replaced every year or so. If a larger cushion was used, it might have been encased in a washable slipcover. Its life would have been extended if it was carried inside on damp nights or when storms broke, but sun quickly faded the limited selection of colors and fabrics available and humidity took its toll in the form of mildew.

Today there are wonderful synthetic fabrics in a wide variety of colors and textures designed to withstand the weather, resist dirt and mildew, and retain their attractive, vibrant colors despite exposure to strong sun. Acrylics are among the most popular of these synthetics. A fabric that looks and feels like cotton, acrylic can be left out on an open porch for the entire season, even in the worst of downpours. When acrylics cover cushions that are made of 100 percent polyester and designed to "drain," both fabric and cushion will dry out in several hours after a thorough soaking and will last for many years. As you shop for upholstered furniture, check tags carefully and accept only solution-dyed acrylics, which guarantee high durability and easy cleaning. Acrylics that are not solution dyed will fade more quickly and lose color altogether if chlorine bleach is used to clean them.

Vinyl-coated polyester, developed about fifteen years ago, has also become a popular choice for porches as well as for decks and patios. A polyester yarn coated with vinyl and woven into attractive, durable open-mesh fabric, it is stain resistant and dries quickly.

Today's modern acrylic fabrics make it possible to use vibrant, exciting colors for porch decorating. Once upon a time, the cheerful colors on these cushions would have been avoided, for fear of fading in the harsh rays of the sun. Happily, new synthetics have largely solved this problem, for upholstery offers softness and comfort and encourages lounging at the end of the day.

Opposite: One of the most important functions a porch fulfills is to carry the outside in, emphasizing views and vistas in the process. The neutral sofa and chairs, piled attractively with comfortable pillows, are arranged to facilitate conversation. The sisal floor covering contrasts easily with the wrought-iron tables, hanging lamp, and patterned screens in this casual, summery environment. Billowing white curtains untie for protection from lakeside breezes. Fancy slipcovered children's chairs, the multifaceted star, and the bust on a pedestal add decorative, interesting touches that celebrate porch living.

On an enclosed porch, there are virtually no furniture limitations. Everything from period pieces to seagrass is appropriate, depending on your preference and how well it "fits" the room. If you're looking to create a casual atmosphere, moiré won't do. If you live where the winters are harsh and prefer to use your porch only three seasons of the year, avoid velvets and heavy brocades.

Color, pattern, and texture all set a mood, so it's important to consider what your essential porch function will be before making selections. Wools and weaves in thicker cottons or linens are matte textured, while the shiny surface of silk and satin, the glaze of chintz, and the directional nap of velvet will catch the light. Fabric can create a luxurious, opulent look or an atmosphere that's comfortable and laid-back, but it's your own sense of style and creativity that will lend uniqueness to your porch and bring enjoyment to family and friends. For example, as autumn and winter approach, wrap cushions in antique shawls, quilts, and kilim rugs for a warm, cozy look. In summer use a crocheted bed coverlet or a light cotton throw to change the atmosphere.

When choosing outdoor furniture, consider the color of your house's exterior, or if it's an enclosed porch, the color of porch walls. Choose furniture that will look good against its intended backdrop. White wicker, for example, may look beautiful in the showroom, but it may disappear against the white exterior of your house. Upholstery should complement the color of the furniture and walls. Dark green is a popular color for outdoor use because it looks cool even on the hottest day and blends subtly with the landscape. Stripes, florals, plaids, checks, brocades, and other patterns are available in dozens of shades. Feel free to use a bolder, more colorful fabric pattern than you would for a living room settee or dining room chair; a cool stripe or lush floral design that would be disconcerting in a living room works beautifully out on the porch.

Dining Tables

It appears that the owners had a single goal in mind for this space and achieved it magnificently. On this gazebolike screened porch, the simple table and chairs allow for a casual, relaxed approach to the dining ritual. The look is spare and uncluttered, despite the decorative trim, finials, and oversized door with stylized border. With the right table settings, fresh-cut or potted flowers, and candles, a simple dinner is a festive occasion.

The rule of the thumb in selecting a table for a dining room is to choose the largest one the room will allow. That's a good rule to follow for the porch as well. You'll revel in the versatility a big table brings. It allows you to entertain lots of friends at one time. There's room for your daughter's entire nursery school class to share the birthday cake. And on rainy summer evenings, you don't have to move the giant jigsaw puzzle you've been working on all day. Instead, you can eat dinner at the far end of the table.

As with chairs and sofas, you can choose from an enormous variety of materials and styles, like wicker, cast or wrought iron, cast aluminum, and of course, wood of every description.

Picnic tables have long been at home on the porch, and nothing says easy living or family get-together better. A sturdy natural or painted redwood picnic table, flanked by backless benches or with simple ladder-back chairs, is a no-nonsense surface for simple meals on the porch. Dress it up with a pair of gingham squares placed on the diagonal, a hand-woven runner down the center, or quilted country place mats.

A plain, plank-topped trestle table is the town cousin of the countrified picnic table. Its scrubbed finish needs no covering, looking dressed for dinner with only the lambent light of hurricane lamps or candles. Cushioned deacon's benches or a row of sturdy painted country chairs will seat dinner guests in style.

If space is at a premium on your porch, use a pair of saw horses and an old flat door or a piece of strong plywood as a table. Once your impromptu table is covered by linens, nobody will be the wiser, and you can store the components in the garage or the basement when not in use. The money you save on the table can be well spent purchasing beautiful tablecloths and dishware.

A Pembroke table—a narrow form with hinged side leaves that prop up on supports—is a useful space saver and can be expanded to accommodate your dinner guests. When not in use it can be folded to its smallest size and placed against a wall or behind a settee.

The casual atmosphere of beach houses and summer cottages lends itself to unusual, quirky furnishings. You might use a giant cable spool (like the ones left behind by telephone or utility companies) turned on its end and painted white as a table for four. Marine rope that has been tightly coiled and neatly tacked in place makes an attractive surface. Or use a gnarled tree trunk topped with a piece of round glass for a rustic dining table.

The quaint effect of white on white and the sunlight flowing through an uninterrupted bank of French doors on this long, narrow porch suggest gracious, old-fashioned living. Afternoon tea is served amid pretty wicker and the heady perfume of select flowering plants.

Right: Long, angled, energy-efficient windows—designed to permit maximum sun and warmth—create a dramatic backdrop on this somewhat unusual dining porch. The long trestle table will readily seat eight to ten people, allowing hosts the luxury of large dinner parties without worrying about elbow room. Retractable window coverings will shield diners from direct sun and limit heat in hot weather; pulled up for evening meals, the tiered panes allow a view of the stars. Colorful spring blooms soften the hardness of steel and slate.

Opposite: thought to promote relaxed conversation, round tables are a favorite for casual breakfasts and brunches. Round tables also have the advantage of fitting comfortably into tiny spaces, like this intimate porch corner.

Above: Even a humble secondhand table can become a prize when it's laid with cozy linen and tucked into the corner of an open-air porch. If you have a small furniture budget for your porch, don't despair. Hunt flea markets and tag sales for items that can be dressed up with linens, slipcovers, or paint.

Above right: Chic beige slipcovers carry these chairs to the height of elegance. The table, with its weighty stone base, stands in stark contrast to the softness surrounding it. The restful monochromatic scheme is broken only by plants, the tile border, and the blue-green tint of the table's glass top.

Bungalow and cottage porches lend themselves easily to vintage kitchen furnishings. Your grandmother's enamel or Formica-topped kitchen table may find a new life on your country porch. For a nostalgic dining setting add simple wooden chairs with seats upholstered in fabric scraps from the thirties and forties. Tablecloths and napkins from the same era provide a finishing touch.

Glass-topped metal tables are also at home on the porch. Styles run from the richly ornate to simple geometric shapes. Team them with matching chairs or use wicker or twig chairs for contrast.

Side Tables, Coffee Tables, and Incidental Tables

For a porch designed as a place of respite, the furnishings must anticipate many needs. If you're looking for tranquillity, comfort, and rejuvenation, your furniture will have to reflect that search.

A generous coffee table in front of a sofa or settee has enough room for piles of magazines or for a hand of solitaire while reserving enough space for a pitcher of lemony iced tea. Novels awaiting a

Dark summer greenery forms a perfect backdrop for the graceful white columns and railings that surround this elegant Victorian-style porch. Simplicity, comfort, and informality were the desired effects in this unpretentious display. Twin tables in a sinuous shape echo the graceful curves of chair backs, inspiring a sense of calm in family and visitors alike. Here is the perfect spot for late afternoon drinks and sparkling conversation.

This unassuming gateleg table can be pulled out and set up, with chairs placed around it, in nothing flat for a friendly game of cards or an arts and crafts project. Humble, well-worn furniture can be as comfortable to slip into as an old sweatshirt, and the pieces here—at least some of which are flea market finds—are meant to be used well and often in this family retreat. Nothing says fussy on this rustic porch; relaxation and good fun take precedence. Binoculars remain nearby, reminding family and friends to enjoy the spectacular birdwatching opportunities offered in this woodland bower.

reader might rest on a side table beside a basket kept stocked with writing paper, envelopes, stamps, and a pen, for those who draw comfort from keeping in touch.

For many families, free-time fun revolves around genial games of Monopoly, Clue, or Parcheesi. Card games like bridge, spades, and hearts, or even thousand-piece jigsaw puzzles are also excellent ways to relax with family and friends. A sturdy table placed in an out-of-the-way corner of the porch readily becomes a game center.

For a whimsical, country effect, adapt an antique wooden wagon, or even a vintage Radio Flyer, as a coffee table. Set it before a quilt-covered settee for truly homey flair, and put bricks, stones, or heavy bean bags around the wheels to prevent it from rolling out of place.

Old trays of rattan, Russian silver, copper, or tin set on simple stands make useful coffee or side tables, as will a large slab of marble placed on wide, decorative cement plinths. You might even res-urrect a child's play table and paint it a bright color or treat it with a faux finish. When the space for a coffee table is narrow, use an old, backless bench instead. Be sure the bench legs are the same length to avoid the possibility of it tipping over. Trunks and small wooden chests also make good space-sav-ing tables. As a bonus, you can store books, games, and other odds and ends inside them.

A table placed between two comfortable chairs encourages conversation and makes a useful place for teacups and tall glass-es alike. Wicker, cast- or wrought-iron, or simple redwood tables do a yeoman's job in this role. A bistro table, perhaps covered with a crisp linen cloth, doubles as a stage for a display of flow-ers and as an ad hoc luncheon table for two.

For convenient storage on the porch, find a spot against a wall for an old pine dresser or chest of drawers. Top it with a vintage linen cloth and a small lamp, then fill it with the necessities of porch living like place mats and coasters, board games, paper fans, and citronella candles. Painting the dresser with exterior paint or varnish will help protect it from damp weather.

A matching rattan coffee and side table perform admirably on this glassed-in porch, providing both gor-geous accents and utilitarian surfaces. The low coffee table stands ready to hold pitchers of cool drinks and plenty of glasses; the side table offers a safe resting place for a ceramic lamp and a vintage duck decoy. Mismatched pil-lows and cushions emphasize the relaxed atmosphere, where the comfort of family and friends reigns supreme.

This somewhat unusual pairing—a fainting couch and an end table of exaggerated proportions—helps create a perfect environment where a child can curl up with a book or play on a rainy day. Easy-care flooring encourages hobbies and crafts and vigorous play with toys and games without fear of ruining delicate floors with marks or spilled drinks. A useful, comfortable space for children to enjoy, this area is elegant enough for adult relaxation as well.

Incidental tables can be fashioned from nearly any low, flat-topped piece of furniture. The obsolete furniture of yesteryear can often find new life as an incidental table. You might find an antique pine icebox or pie safe, an Adirondack pine-plank bench, a seed-sorting table with a low railing around three sides, or a vintage butcher's block at a flea market or barn sale. Use your imagination to assimilate these charming pieces into your porch furnishings.

Cupboards and Étagères

Decorators will often use tall pieces of furniture to add variations in height to a room's appearance. Your porch, too, will benefit from that little design trick. Cupboards and étagères—sets of open shelves used for displaying small objects—will not only bring some vertical interest to the space but will also provide you with room to show off your treasures.

Étagères are made using just about every material that other furniture is constructed of, so you will have lots of choices when you begin your search. A wicker étagère will, of course, complement a wicker seating arrangement while metal examples afford a more eclectic look. Many manufacturers of cast-metal furniture include étagères in their lines.

Place an étagère near your dining area on the porch and use it as a sideboard when serving alfresco meals. You can also use your étagère to store decorative platters and trays, pitchers, glassware, and bar supplies.

A baker's rack also works well to hold board games, magazines, books, and other family-time essentials. Use a pretty lidded basket or a hinged wooden box on one of the shelves to store playing cards, dice, poker chips, and other small items. Or use your baker's rack to keep crafts supplies and projects organized and close at hand.

Set for an elegant afternoon tea, a makeshift plywood table draped with a floral tablecloth is a beautiful counterpoint to the wonderful Welsh cupboard at the rear. The lower cabinets of the piece are fitted with locks, providing safe storage for cherished collectibles when the family is out of town.

B u i l t - I n P i e c e s

The types of built-ins you plan for your porch are limited only by your imagination. There are numerous projects to be found in books and magazines, and many of them include construction plans. These do-it-yourself projects range from benches and planters to bookshelves, storage cabinets, and bed platforms, but it's essential to first make an assessment of your needs. If your porch will be used primarily for relaxation, built-in floor planters or window boxes would be a pleasant touch. Depending on your space, you might line one of the walls of your porch with built-in benches, perhaps covered with a long, custom-made cushion. Often benches can be built so that the seats lift up, revealing storage space for cushions and kids' games, puzzles, and toys. Recessed shelving can add to the beauty of your porch and offer a place to display plants or various artifacts.

If you're planning to use your porch for dining and entertaining, a long sideboard hinged onto the wall would be most helpful when serving. When not in use, the piece can fold up to conserve space. A built-in bar with cabinets above and below is ideal for storing glassware intended for use on the porch, saving lots of steps and work.

Cases and chests are components that do double duty. They give you new storage capacity and function as furniture at the same time. If you're handy, these can be built easily out of softwood lumber or plywood, with or without face frames and backs. Doors, counter surfaces, and pedestals are all additional options that will make the pieces both more attractive and more useful. Paint them or seal them with a natural wood finish to make them an integral part of your porch decor. The wide range of choices for built-ins gives you plenty of opportunity to mix and match the elements according to your own scheme.

Opposite: A built-in bench incorporated into the wall of this porch creates an appealing niche for a cozy heart-to-heart between friends or a well-deserved afternoon siesta. Nestled beneath the window, a shelf filled with potted flowers and greenery recalls an old-fashioned window box. The walls and chairs have been sponged a captivating periwinkle; a Southwest flavor prevails in the style and pattern of the blanket and throw pillow and the wrought-iron wall decoration.

CHAPTER FOUR

Finishing Touches

Above: A box planter stamped with a star motif, oversized wrought-iron art, a hollowed-out tree limb candle, and lettuce leaf dishes may not be the right detailing for the living room, but on the porch this whimsical collection delights the eye and contributes a sense of the unexpected.

Left: Decorative details make all the difference in this comfortable outdoor living room. Fresh flowers and a heavy glass paperweight—a blessing on the sometimes windy porch—bring genteel charm to the rustic coffee table. A heavy sculpture rests atop a sturdy wooden pedestal, visually balancing the furniture, which has been placed to take advantage of the view.

Roof, floor, and railings and rockers and settees may be the staples of the porch, but accessories are the spice. In this chapter we'll look at a the role of collectibles and accessories, including pillows, throws, and quilts. We'll also explore ways to add shade, privacy, and protection from the elements with awnings, louvers, drapery, and plantings.

Decorating with Collectibles

Opposite: Cherished pieces like this twenty-one-drawer oak chest, antique water jars, and a painting of sentimental value add character to a Southwest-style veranda. The wall lantern—which is in keeping with the nature of the outdoor space—sheds necessary light. These elements blend beautifully on the enclosed porch, while palm fronds, begonias, and a delicate, flowering vine soften the sun's rays to a gentle glow.

Bring some of your favorite collectibles—folk art carvings, Depression glass, baskets, paperweights, or tole pieces—outside on the porch and display them. A finely crafted game board, such as one for backgammon or chess also makes a beautiful statement and serves a practical purpose as well.

Baskets can be filled with magazines, flowers, or handiwork to provide attractive storage as well as a carefree country feel. If your porch will be used as a play space, consider a hamper-sized basket or a wicker blanket chest to serve as a repository for the toys that are sure to accumulate.

Select pieces of glassware contribute immeasurable charm to your coffee and side tables, and hold cool drinks, candy, or snacks. Tea services, vases, and candlesticks are other pragmatic pieces that also have supreme decorative value on the porch.

Art collections featuring folk paintings on wood, hand-painted pottery, or stone sculpture are also appropriate for the porch. Do consider, before you remove your prized pieces to the out-of-doors, how damp conditions will affect them. The porch is not the best place for treasured oil paintings or other delicate artwork. To be entirely sure that your art will be safe from the weather on your porch, you might select pieces intended for use as garden accents.

Anything you cherish will be a welcome addition to your porch, and will enhance your mood by creating warm, pleasant surroundings. Make sure, though, that the pieces you leave on your porch are not too valuable and that the space is relatively secure—the porch's outdoor nature leaves it somewhat vulnerable.

Pillows and Throws

While furniture can be traced back to ancient Chinese dynasties and the pharaohs of Egypt, pillows or cushions of some sort—pads of fur wrapped around straw, small twigs, or leaves—were very likely the first form of home furnishing ever used. Since that time, pillows have carried crowns for coronations, and have appeared on thrones, chairs, benches, beds, floors, and windowsills.

Out on the porch, once your sofas, chairs, tables, and plants have been placed, the artful arrangement of pillows and throws can contribute a comfortable, homey touch to your decor. Pillows and decorative throws will also add color, pattern, texture, and detail to your porch. So when a cozy, inviting outdoor room is your goal, add as many pillows and throws as you can.

Use pillows on your porch to maximize the comfort of your chairs and sofas. Masses of plump pillows piled on a sofa make an exceptionally inviting spot, while several large pillows on the floor can be fun for children to use while playing board games or as a nap time incentive.

If you plan to leave your pillows out on an open air or screened porch, look for special weatherproof acrylic fabrics. These are now available in a wide variety of stripes, florals, and solids that will match or contrast with your porch furnishings, depending on your tastes. If your porch is enclosed or you don't mind carting pillows in during storms or at night, use any fabric that catches your eye. Heavy tapestry or fine needlepoint, vintage linens or cheerful gingham, bright chintz or classic lace—all have their special charms and can be used to great effect on your porch. If you are adept with a sewing machine (or know someone who is) you might try making pillows from worn flannel sheets or shirts for a cozy country flavor. Use faded quilt remnants for another favorite country look.

Opposite: Sunday afternoon is a special time to relax, put one's feet up, and linger over the paper in a verdant setting. Neutral-toned pillows and a creamy lap robe make this slat-backed chaise a comfortable spot even on chilly days. The stone planter is a weatherproof take on a magazine basket, and efficiently prevents the newspapers from becoming strewn about the floor.

No-nonsense plaid pillows effectively temper the sweetness of these splashy floral sofa and chair cushions. When coordinating fabrics, make sure that one has a simple pattern and shares its predominant color with the contrasting fabric. Here, the dark green of the subtle plaid picks up the foliage in the busy floral pattern as well as the color of the wicker, making for a smoothly sophisticated match.

Collect interesting remnants from fabric and decorating stores to have made into incidental pillows. Mattress ticking, too, is an inexpensive, practical material for pillows, and you can use the money you save to splurge on an interesting piping to trim them with. Look for vintage table and bed linens at flea markets, yard sales, and white elephant sales. Even pieces with stains and tears can be cut up to make a pile of lovely pillows with the flavor of yesteryear.

For an electric style, make pillows from nautical flags, Indian bedspreads, tablecloths from the thirties, or even a batik sarong or an old kimono. Varying the sizes, shapes, textures, and colors will add style and interest to your porch decor. Check the resource section on page 142 to find how-to books on designing and making pillows without sewing.

Piles of pristine ivory pillows, punctuated by splashes of autumnal color in the guise of accent pillows and a throw, offer a sincere invitation to sit back and relax. The view is nearly irresistible, and together with the lush arrangement of pillows, guarantees hours of dreamy contemplation.

Most often we think of the porch as a summertime place, but an early spring morning or cool October afternoon spent sitting out on a rocker, wrapped in a warm blanket, can be delightful and inspirational. Look for pale, loosely woven mohairs or thin, warm-weather quilts in muted colors for chilly late-summer days. Heavier wool throws in vibrant stripes or plaids and Navajo or Mexican blankets are ideal for colder weather.

Fold a baby-soft woven wool coverlet over the back of a wicker settee to pull over your shoulders when the sun goes down. Or place a bold plaid stadium blanket on the back of a sturdy wooden rocker to add color and warmth. When it's warm but buggy, a light, gauzy throw can serve as a sort of wraparound mosquito netting without adding weight or unwanted heat. Small throws or even baby quilts can double as tablecloths while large throws, draped over a chair or settee, serve admirably as impromptu slipcovers.

Swings and Hammocks

The delightful old-fashioned wicker porch swing, a throwback to simpler, more relaxed times, is piled with pillows for a look that says, "come sit awhile." Everything here is quietly comfortable and subdued, without clutter or undue distraction. A rolling tea cart stands by to provide ready refreshment, while greenery in pots and hanging planters provides beauty and scent.

Accessories like swings and hammocks can make your porch seem like a little slice of heaven. A swing hung from the ceiling offers escape from the day's stresses, even as it adds old-fashioned charm and a measure of nostalgia. Hammocks, on the other hand, recreate the leisurely atmosphere of a tropical isle. Both swings and hammocks are the ultimate places to relax and refresh one's spirit. They're also wonderful if you have children. A porch swing is a perfect place to calm a fussy baby or read to a young child. Older kids have a ball swinging back and forth in a hammock on a lazy afternoon.

The old-fashioned porch swing has made a dramatic comeback, as people seek new roads to a more relaxing lifestyle. Set apart from the intimate conversation area on this wide-columned porch, the swing is an irresistible pleasure, offering a spot away from the crowd or an opportunity to read, needlepoint, or simply take in the beauty of the surroundings.

Antique porch swings are not too easy to find and if you do come across one, chances are good that it will need a great deal of rebuilding. Reproductions of antique porch swings are more widely available, through catalogues specializing in garden furniture or items for outdoor living. By the mid-1800s, porch swings were enormously popular and this trend lasted well into the twentieth century. Some of these swings were simple, homemade contraptions built from scraps of lumber. Others had more carefully constructed forms of wicker, rush, or cane, or boasted wooden slats in a basket-weave pattern.

The high gloss of the hardwood floor on this open-air porch is an object of beauty in and of itself. The Adirondack chair in the foreground and the porch swing, its country cousin, at the far end of the porch are made to look ever so inviting with friendly yellow cushions and throw pillows. Regal columns and airy blooms spilling out of pots and jardinieres are also basic elements of this porch's appeal.

Earlier in this century, canvas hammocks with fringed sides graced shady corners of country porches. The Victorians were also fond of fringed hammocks and, in the spirit of decorative excess that characterized nineteenth-century furnishings, some of the fringes were so long that they nearly brushed the floor. Paisley and cotton print pillows filled the hammock to overflow, assuring plenty of comfort.

Hammocks made in the Yucatan area of Mexico are hand-strung and knotted of colorful cotton fibers. These showy, lightweight hammocks can easily be hung on a pair of hooks on a shady part of the porch for an afternoon's snooze, then removed to make room for other activities.

Just looking at a hammock can evoke soothing images. Casting a glance at the porch hammock while backing out the driveway in the morning, bound for work and a stressful day, can lower blood pressure, ease tension, and inspire positive thinking. This classic Hatteras hammock is so popular because it gets high marks for both comfort and durability.

The Hatteras hammock, a classic cotton rope hammock well known for its award-winning, hand-crafted design, is still the most popular hammock on the market. Available in 100 percent cotton or 100 percent polyester, these hammocks are known for strength, durability, and quality of workmanship.

Most hammocks are sized for one but they are also made in sizes wide enough to accommodate two or three people. When making buying decisions, you may want to consider a hammock with a tighter weave, which will offer increased support for your body and not stretch and sag as much as looser styles. And always make sure it's fitted with a pillow so you can nap in comfort. Metal or wood hammock stands are readily available if your porch doesn't offer an ideal spot for hanging a hammock.

A w n i n g s

Outdoor living areas can be transformed by the cooling shade of an awning. Here, the awning goes beyond usefulness, as decorative edges add interest and style to the setting. A straw rug breaks up the expanse of cool stone underfoot; Adirondack chairs mix easily with other pieces in this informal tableaux.

From vacation cottages at the seashore to houses throughout the suburban landscape, it's an unmistakable sign of summer when the awnings are hung out. An awning can shade and cool a porch, deflecting the warm afternoon sun and making it possible to sit a bit longer on a lazy day or enjoy a late lunch

Tenting material, complete with portable decking—presented here in the ever-popular bright yellow stripe—can be used to enclose a patio area, creating a wonderful, protected porch environment. Roll-down plastic is ready to prevent rainstorms or strong gusts from spoiling a relaxing afternoon or a small party. Comfortable seating, plenty of reading material, and an abundance of plants and flowers create a pulled-together look in this temporary summertime living area.

or an early dinner in comfort. For many porch owners, an awning is both a necessity and an aesthetically pleasing element. It can create the look and feel of coolness and at the same time add immeasurably to the beauty of a home.

Preservationists Renee Kahn and Ellen Meagher found in their research that canvas was first used for awnings in the late 1700s, when striped fabric was used to cover entry porches. Not too much later, sheet metal was painted in awning stripes to look like fabric awnings, but these metal awnings had the advantage of a sturdier form. By the early part of the twentieth century, many houses were designed

with awnings as part of the overall plan, and as Kahn and Meagher point out, the removal of the awnings by subsequent owners eliminated a vital finishing touch.

In the late nineteenth and early twentieth centuries, awnings were usually dark colors—green or blue—with vertical stripes. Although the colors were fairly uniform, there was diversity in the stripes. Some sported combinations of wide and narrow widths, giving the impression of gradations in color. Other awnings had one wide stripe placed every three feet or so. Grander homes might feature extravagant awning treatments complete with swags and fringes. Many fancy awnings boasted scalloped edging, while plainer styles were simply squared off.

Most residential awnings today are made of canvas, though lately acrylics have grown somewhat in popularity. Unlike canvas, acrylics feature the fabric design on both sides. Aluminum is a third choice, but this type of awning is most often used for commercial purposes or as pull-down hurricane protection.

Though awnings are available in a variety of solid colors and stripes, research shows that nearly 50 percent of consumers choose either a solid green awning or one with green-and-white stripes. Despite the fact that there are approximately five hundred other shades to choose from, most people still prefer the "traditional" colors and style. The awnings on most residences are characterized by a triangle-shaped panel on their sides.

Awnings are fitted with galvanized steel frames that home owners can expect to last as long as twenty years. Generally speaking, awnings are a good investment for your home and are made to hold up well for many years if they are cared for properly. Most essential is proper winterizing; awnings must be removed from windows or porches at the end of the season. Take them down only when they are dry and store them in a dry place when not in use.

Opposite: An awning can shade an open-air deck from the searing effects of the sun and offer protection from the elements in a way that is both stylish and sensible. All-weather green wicker helps create the illusion of coolness, while mixed florals, prints, stripes, and patchwork add personality. The artful placement of plants and favorite knickknacks completes the picture.

Sun-Filtering Shades, Drapery, and Louvers

Above: Sun-filtering latticework used overhead and carried over to the side wall provides privacy and causes a sensuous dappling of the light. In open porch areas, where too-bright sunshine makes it impossible to use the porch during the heat of the day, lattice material can be a quick and effective solution.

Opposite: An educated mix of rattan and wicker furniture, patchwork quilting, a modern acrylic floral print, and cool blue stripes offers eye appeal and, surprisingly, a quiet balance despite the rather frenzied variety. The drapery, an unexpected element, is simply hung from a white steel rod, and readily provides privacy in this attractive setting.

You've built or restored a beautiful porch. It's furnished with things you've selected with great care, one at a time. Technically speaking, the project has been completed, yet it still needs something to turn it into a truly finished area. You want to introduce a softness and take the hard edges off the bright sun that can age the furnishings, not to mention your skin. You can do just that with shades, drapery, or louvers.

For draperies, choose light fabrics like lace, cheesecloth, and scrim, which drape effortlessly, look breezy and soft, and filter harsh midday sun. Experiment with folding and gathering the fabric in a variety of ways to create a languid, tropical mood. Many window treatments can be tacked up or knotted around large nails or special hardware placed at the corners of your windows. Porch living is casual, so forgo formal pleats, tight ruffles, and complicated constructions. Be sure to choose washable fabrics that are easy to launder rather than heavy brocades that need dry cleaning or polished cottons that will require ironing. Avoid somber, dark drapery and fussy valances—these will give your porch a stuffy, heated look.

Shades and louvers can effectively control sun exposure, blocking the sun entirely or admitting measured streams of light. In years past, there was little choice in decorative shades and louvers but today the options are practically endless. In addition to roller shades—which can be reverse-rolled in order to put the roller at the back, giving the fabric facing the room its trimmest finish—there are several variations of roman shades and balloon shades. Shades can splash color onto your porch or, in neutral tones, can simply fade into the background. Louvers, which provide a spare, clean appearance, are available in horizontal and vertical styles in wood, aluminum, vinyl, and a wide selection of fabrics.

U m b r e l l a s

Large, wide-striped umbrellas are summer objects. They bring us back to the seashore vacations of our childhood, resurrecting images of happy, carefree days. The cool, crisp stripes used here complement the slatted table and chairs, even as its octagonal expanse offers shelter from the relentless sun. The geometric painted rug picks up the colors of the umbrella, as do checked cloths that line baskets of summer fruits. Use an umbrella only if a porch is spacious, and select only light, airy fabrics that repel the sun. Round tables, which are especially conducive to conversation, are the most popular table shapes.

On the right porch, an umbrella can create the illusion of a sunny summer day even in cool springtime weather. Such an accessory will only work on a spacious porch, perhaps the "L" of a wraparound porch or on a terrace adjoining a glassed-in porch. If the space is at all cramped, the umbrella will only reinforce feelings of claustrophobia.

An umbrella can create a cool spot, providing relief from the sun's strongest rays. At night, with twinkling lights set up high in the ribs, it can cast a lovely glow over a perfect dinner.

Umbrellas are available in several shapes—round, oval, octagonal, rectangular, or square. Let your table's shape and size determine the umbrella you place above it. Round tables and umbrellas are the most sought after, since they promote an intimate atmosphere and require a bit less space than square or rectangular models.

Umbrellas also come in a variety of colors, fabrics, and constructions. Open-weave materials gently filter the sun and let warm air flow out while those designed with opaque fabric offer the best protection from the sun.

The most common sizes for garden umbrellas are seven and a half and eight and a half feet (2.3 and 2.6m) in diameter, though they are available in smaller or larger sizes. These big, showy umbrellas are usually seen with fringe or a scalloped finish around the edges. The pole is most often made of aluminum (a material that withstands weather well) and is equipped with a mechanism that allows the umbrella to tilt, offering increased protection from the sun. A crank in the pole opens and closes the umbrella with ease.

Finishing Touches

Market umbrellas, similar to the ones used by European street vendors to shade their fruits and vegetables, are available now with poles and ribs of aluminum or resin and with covers in a variety of colors and fabrics. The original style of market umbrellas, which had natural-colored canvas tops supported by poles and ribs of wood, is still a favorite choice. Some now open and close with cranks, while others must be opened by hand.

An appropriate umbrella base is essential to safety and must be chosen carefully. The weight of the base must be sufficient to hold the umbrella in place; otherwise, both the umbrella and the table will be easily blown over in a gust of wind.

A sporty umbrella in blue-and-white stripes offers shady respite for a solitary sunbather on this beach house porch. The heavy, square, iron umbrella stand ensures against the vagaries of ocean breezes. Painted white, the base matches flawlessly the clean lines and basic color scheme of its surroundings.

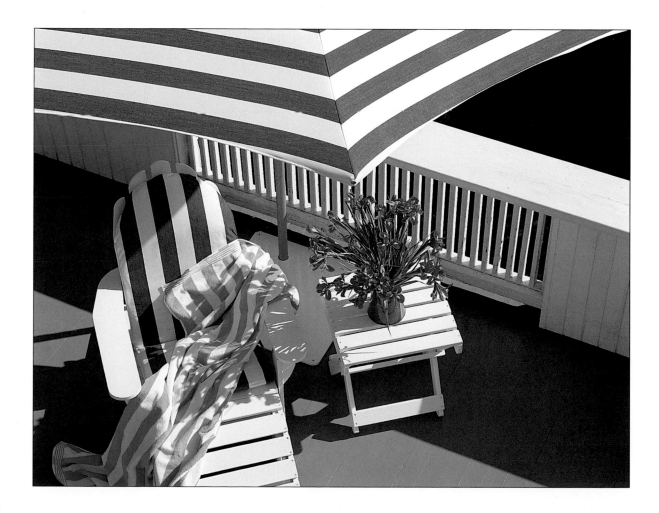

CHAPTER FIVE

Plantings for the Porch and Beyond

Trees, shrubs, vines, and flowers add color, privacy, interest,

and plain old-fashioned enjoyment to porch living. They soften

the hard edges of porch structures, perfume the air, and create

riotous masses of color or restful patches of cool, monochro-

matic greens.

Above: Decorating a porch shouldn't be a serious business. It is perhaps the one place where fantasies may be indulged and eccentricities celebrated. This delightful trio of vintage watering cans hung high up near the ceiling is useful and decorative all at once. Their handy placement makes it easy to pull one down to revive a thirsty plant.

Left: For many people, the view from a porch is just as important as the decor of the structure itself. Here, the owners placed gardens so that their bounty could be savored throughout the season. From the sheltered side porch, views of exuberant black-eyed Susans and graceful daylilies make for a particularly pleasant contrast with the dark greens of the lawn and mature trees.

Above: Grouping painted terra-cotta pots of dwarf evergreens near the doorway creates a warmly welcoming walkway. These sturdy sentinels give a full, balanced look to an entrance, and are most attractive against the white railing and dark floor of this porch.

Above right: The classic beauty of this traditional home is enhanced by its graceful wraparound porch. The right foundation plantings are essential in maintaining curb appeal and a tidy, well-kept appearance. Plantings that climb too high limit views from the porch and obscure the beauty of a home; evergreen plantings grown tall and leggy will darken and bring winter gloom to front rooms.

Gardening

Whether you're known for your extraordinary houseplants or for your lavish backyard garden, a small porch—screened or open—makes an ideal place to practice your craft. Here you can prepare cut flowers, pot and prune houseplants, shelter outdoor containers in winter, start seeds and cuttings in the spring, and make handcrafted gifts from the garden's bounty.

Because this is a working space—a place that by its nature will be messy and dirty at times—you will most likely want to use a back or side porch, preferably one that is well away from daily traffic and interruptions.

Everything is quietly comfortable in the warm glow of dappled sunshine. The sun's rays reflect quite nicely on the arched trellis structure that rises above the wide mixed border. An ambitious vine has already scrambled up both sides of the trellis, promising to further enhance the colors and textures of the annuals and perennials that spread beneath it. Broken slate laid informally leads visitors to the front entrance of this authentic country home. The granite duck is squarely placed to face visitors, offering a silent yet friendly welcome.

To turn your porch into a private garden center, outfit it with a workbench or an old plank-top table, and add shelves or cupboards for storing pots, planters, potting soil, and fertilizers. Hang your large tools from big wooden or wrought-iron hooks and keep smaller tools handy in a bucket or basket.

Having running water on your garden porch is extremely helpful, so talk to your plumber about the feasibility of installing a small sink near your work surface or in a convenient corner. For extra charm, search architectural remnant stores and salvage yards for an old copper or shallow stone sink like those found in early farmhouses. They work especially well for gardening projects, as they are usually roomy and their beauty is only enhanced by a bit of soil and some weathering.

This delightful profusion of summer blooms displayed in a simple milk pitcher brings the garden onto the porch. Beyond the latticework, a cutting garden infuses the view with color and the air with perfume. The porch is the perfect spot for arranging flowers; for cleanup you will have only to sweep clipped stems and leaves off the porch.

If your garden room is heated, it will function much like a greenhouse. If it isn't heated, think about installing some kind of heating system. What you use for heat will depend on how cold the winters are in your part of the country. New, highly efficient electric units might work for you, or explore the possibility of a propane or gas heater.

Here, vines make all the difference, bringing a vertical dimension to planting. Their emerald green color adds old-fashioned charm to this pergola-roofed porch. Twirling over and around porch columns, a vine can soften a severe structure and cover damaged or discolored brick, less-than-pleasing drainpipes, and more. If this vine is coaxed to crawl over the top boards, bright sunshine will be softly filtered, extending the enjoyable hours of the porch.

Softening and Overlaying Hard Structures

As with skillfully applied makeup, flowers and plants can accent a prominent feature, play down a blemish, and in general, improve a porch's appearance with color, texture, and shaping. If your porch is part of the front of your house, flowers and plants will make a personal statement about you, calling out a welcome long before you know visitors have arrived.

Dark green vines trained on an arbor fashion a roof for this patio space, converting it easily into a shady porch. The red brick floor provides warm color in contrast to the cool greens and whites of plants and furniture. Bent-twig chairs are the perfect choice in this nature-inspired setting.

Hydrangeas or geraniums potted up and placed in rows on the far edges of the steps leading up to your porch can soften and ornament an entrance. A large expanse of flooring can be transformed from bare to beautiful with groupings of planters and urns overflowing with colorful summer blooms. A trailing, flamboyant clematis can twine its stems up and around a railing, window, or drainpipe, making even the most prosaic structure into a romantic trellis. The pendant blossoms of wisteria planted near an entrance give

Glorious, fragrant wisteria is truly one of spring's showstoppers. Here the vine is shown at its peak, dressing up the corner of an old-fashioned columned porch. Low, monochromatic foundation plantings are a perfect counterpoint to such flamboyance. Great care was obviously taken in planning this springtime display. Set chairs in the vicinity to further enjoy wisteria's delicious scent.

the porch a cool look on a scorching afternoon, and Boston or English ivy or Virginia creeper provide a pleasing greenness as they spill out from foundation plantings or climb up walls and over porch screens.

Keep in mind that a big show of a single, vivid color against a contrasting background becomes a dramatic focal point and directly draws the eye. You might place a quartet of terra-cotta pots filled with hot pink petunias against a white wall or a huge tub of pure white nicotiana in front of a dark shutter, or a position a lush, dark green fern with the sky as a backdrop.

In true Queen Anne style, this porch is filled with an extravagance of plants and artifacts. There is no focal point in this friendly confusion, as blooms burst forth from stately jardinieres, plastic pots, window boxes, and Victorian plant stands. Who knows what manner of flaws are hidden by this profusion of greenery? Potted plants and vines cheerfully hide peeling paint, holes in walls, and other imperfections on your porch.

You can also use flowers and greenery to pull attention away from a compromised view or an unsightly architectural flaw. Plant standards, topiaries, and bowls of freshly cut, colorful flowers on tables will distract from less-than-perfect walls or moldings. Set boxes of textured plants like velvety pansies, waxy ivies, or stiff yuccas under windows or on the floor next to the swing to move the eye away from the cracked concrete or to cover peeling paint.

If the hard area you need to soften is too large for a few potted plants to tackle, try growing vines and climbers on trellises. Plant them in the garden outside the porch and train them up a trellis attached to porch walls or railings, or place the plants in large pots equipped with small trellises. Morning glories, scarlet runner beans, mandevilla, ivies, hop vines, clematis, and potato vines are all good candidates for this role.

Creating Garden Rooms

With gardening now the fastest-growing pastime, those who love spending time planting flowers and vegetables are expanding their gardening venues to include garden rooms, and porches across the country are being converted to that cause.

A serene, almost Zenlike atmosphere prevails on this open-air porch. Ceramic, wood, stone, lush greenery, and feathery ferns combine to create a perfect place for conversation or meditation. Retreat to this space to contemplate plans for next year's garden; the view of the current garden offers points for comparison and encourages flights of gardening fancy.

Depending on the climate, garden rooms needn't be enclosed. This peaceful ground-level porch, which serves as a sort of outdoor sitting room, is bounded only by palm fronds, clinging vines, and pots of cacti. The immediacy of being able to step right out onto the grass adds a new dimension to the garden room.

An enclosed porch or sunroom makes an ideal garden room, especially if it opens onto the terrace and yard. Here is the perfect place to pore over seed and plant catalogs, search for inspiration from gardening books, and tend your seedlings.

Whether it's an antique conservatory, old-fashioned glassed-in porch, or open-air space, a garden room affords you an intimacy with flowers and foliage. And there are fewer more restorative or restful places than a comfortable room that brings the garden "indoors."

A garden room can be as nostalgic as a fern-filled Victorian glass conservatory or as exotic as a hothouse filled with tropical plants. Or your green space can speak directly of your horticultural interests—as intense or as casual as they may be.

An enchanting spot for afternoon tea, this open-air porch offers ample reason to linger a bit longer. Lush foliage nearly encircles the space, forming an airy outdoor room. Terra-cotta floor tiles are perfect for a space designed to hold lots of plants; you can water without worrying about stains and discoloration. Dappled sunlight plays over French bistro chairs and a table decked with a gaily printed cloth. So simple to set up, this alfresco repast provides an afternoon's worth of guaranteed enjoyment.

Use colors for fabric and furniture that feel like a garden to you. For some that means whites, pinks, blues, and yellows. Others will choose shades of green. Flowery chintz prints, awning stripes, or simple mattress ticking make good choices for cushions and pillows, but do keep in mind the fading power of the sun.

Terra-cotta, slate, brick, or composition flooring makes sense since you'll be watering plants here. Sisal or rush matting is also an appropriate choice, and has the advantage of a neutral, natural look. Install simple curtains, canvas shades, match stick or wooden venetian blinds, or shutters so you can control the light on too-bright days.

Arrange a pretty sitting area with a pair of white or dark green wicker chairs. An overstuffed chaise covered with a floral print makes a great place to relax while you daydream about next year's bloom-

For many people, a porch is a place to relax, unwind, and get a breath of fresh air. For others, it's a play area for children, a place to entertain, or the perfect spot to start seedlings. But of all its varied uses, dining is perhaps the most pleasant; breakfast, brunch, and intimate late suppers are all the more memorable when served in the relaxed ambience of an outdoor room filled with plants and garden furniture. A proper dining table and chairs are most unnecessary. Pull wicker chairs and benches around a makeshift table spread with a colorful cloth, set with your best china, and enjoy.

ing season. Add a quirky piece for unique charm; an old wooden reclining steamer chair or a striped canvas beach chaise is a perfect choice. Keep catalogs and books nearby in a big splint basket, an old wooden toolbox, or a clean rectangular terra-cotta or cast-cement planter.

Start a collection of vintage or reproduction plant stands and étagères and fill them with ferns, ivy topiaries, orchids, annuals salvaged from the summer terrace garden, or tender houseplants. Wire, wicker, and cast-iron étagères and bakers' racks are perfect for lush displays of your favorite plants.

Add a ceiling fan to keep the air circulating, and include some recessed lighting and a discreet floor lamp for evening reading. Then fill your porch garden room with plants and more plants.

Planting for Color and Fragrance

When you take the time to plan for scent and color, your porch will easily become the most pleasant room in the house. Though our sense of smell is the least understood of all the senses, it is well known that the phenomenon of scent imprinting occurs throughout our lives. The aroma of a certain cologne, for instance, will bring back vivid memories of our teen years while the smell of the seashore can recall in an instant a family vacation that happened half a lifetime ago.

Practically speaking, a garden planted for fragrance needs warm stillness and sheltered conditions, but not too much heat. Hot and dry conditions can rob flowers of scent, while humidity, the thing most of us hate about the summer, actually encourages garden fragrances. A breezy porch near the seashore or beside a mountain lake may be a perfect spot to cool off, but it's the wrong place for a fragrance garden. Scents will simply disperse on this type of porch. Still air and humid conditions are absolute requirements for getting the most out of the fragrant plantings surrounding your porch. In fact, a rainy day is the time when your garden will have the most scent, and it's a wonderful time to be on the porch too.

Begin planning for scent around the perimeter of your porch by choosing fragrant foundation plantings. A mock orange introduces delicate

What could epitomize summer more beautifully than this incredible display of hydrangeas in full bloom? Set in beds surrounding the porches of this meticulously restored Victorian home, the flowers of these mature bushes recall nothing so much as huge scoops of sherbet. The authentic palette of the house combines with these singular blooms for a stunning celebration of pinks, purples, and blues.

white flowers and sweet scent, Carolina allspice imparts a potent fragrance, and viburnums bear fruit that attracts birds and showy flowers that infuse the air with a spicy scent. *Clethra*, also known as summersweet, and *Chimonanthus*, whose common name is wintersweet, are both good shrubs for a scented garden.

Gardenias and daphnes, both southern favorites, are also known for their heady fragrance. And anyone who has visited England's famed Exbury or Leonardslee gardens when the rhododendrons and azaleas are in bloom knows of the glorious aromas these plants offer.

For vertical interest along with scent, encourage a honeysuckle (the strongly scented, white-flowered form 'Halliana' is a good choice) to climb up a railing, drainpipe, or trellis. Sweet autumn clematis is a wonderfully scented vine to tie up near seating areas. Romantic, purple wisteria is another fragrant favorite, as are butterfly bushes, sweet peas, herbaceous peonies, irises, and lilies of the valley.

Nicotiana (flowering tobacco) may be used as an annual bedding plant for daytime color, but since it depends on night-flying moths for pollination, its perfume can be enjoyed in the evening. Other highly scented annuals include stocks, four o'clocks, and cornflowers.

For aromas ranging from apple blossom, lemon, and licorice to peppermint, pineapple, and chocolate, plant scented geraniums in pots on the porch. Hanging planters full of scented geraniums are also an inspired idea, since they'll scent the air at standing height. While scented geraniums have tiny, nondescript flowers, their soft, slightly fuzzy leaves emit wonderful smells when they are rubbed lightly.

If you have the patience, try growing tuberoses, a tender bulb. Their fragrance is so beautiful that the flowers are cultivated commercially as an ingredient for perfume. But they can be finicky; you need to plant them indoors in early spring if you live in a cold climate, and they take months until they bloom. The scented reward, however, is well worth the wait.

Opposite: This tiny front garden—with its old-fashioned, small-town look—presents a friendly face to passersby. The white picket fence twined with ivy and the charming curbside garden are unmistakably welcoming. This plan extends the small gardening space of the front yard to the strip of ground that borders the sidewalk. In most homes this spot is simply planted with grass, but here a variety of thriving plants turns the space into the narrowest of gardens.

Opposite: A wonderful way to make use of backyard space, this charming garden with its decorative fencing cuts lawn maintenance and provides ready access to a variety of fabulous blooms. An informal garden that mixes perennials, annuals, and herbs, it offers a pleasing view from any of the house's four porches.

Sweet-scented shrub roses planted in large pots and set out on the porch perfume the air beautifully and are lovely to look at. Some cultivars known for their scent include the damask roses 'Jacques Cartier' and 'Petit Lisette', the gallica rose 'Jenny Duval', and the Bourbon rose 'Louise Odier'.

Although their blooms don't last nearly long enough, the exquisite flowers of Oriental lilies are perfumed with an intoxicating, exotic scent. Plant them in a bed near the porch, or put them in big pots in a sunny spot on the porch. You may want to remove the pot after the lilies have bloomed because the foliage does not remain attractive. The most highly scented cultivars are pure white 'Casa Blanca', crimson and white 'Star Gazer', and pink and white 'Rubrum'.

For wonderful fragrance and somewhat unusual color, try a black cosmos for chocolate scents, and match it with vanilla-scented heliotrope. Alyssum and trailing lobelia provide a white and purple-blue tumble of color as well as delicious scents.

Color preference is highly subjective and with flowering plants you can have your choice. Achieve riotous colors with cerise and lavender petunias, golden-yellow calceolarias, annual carnations, fuchsia, and cool, silvery white–leaved cinerarias. Plant salmon-pink petunias backed by fuchsia bells a shade deeper for a pastel palette, then add marguerites, sweet alyssum, and lavender-pink ageratums. Explore new color combinations with annuals in pots—it's an easy and inexpensive way to experiment with a nearly limitless palette of flower colors.

Many gardeners achieve great success using foliage plants for an exciting array of color. On a shady porch, plant fancy-leafed calidiums, whose colors are glorious combinations of pinks, silver, greens, and white, or pot up coleus for a kaleidoscope of color. *Hypoestes*, or polka dot plant, puts forth an enchanting combination of green, pink, and cream-colored leaves.

Following is a list of plants that do well in window boxes:

- *boxwood*
- *chrysanthemum*
- *cyclamen*
- *fuchsia*
- *lobelia*
- *marigold*
- *miniature roses*
- *nasturtiums*
- *snapdragon*
- *sweet alyssum*
- *thrift*
- *verbena*

W i n d o w   B o x e s

It's amazing how just a few well-placed window boxes, filled to the brim with plants and flowers, can make your porch immediately feel like home. First you have to make an assessment of your porch and your home to determine whether window boxes are right for your scheme. Some porches will be cluttered rather than enhanced by window boxes.

An open porch that sweeps across the front of your house, encompassing both living room and dining room windows, might benefit visually by affixing boxes to each of these windows. You might also consider the open spaces above porch railings as "windows" of a sort and attach boxes at railing level for an especially summery gardenlike ambiance. Or place window boxes atop the porch railing, either in a continuous line or strategically spaced, to create a lovely backdrop for reading, relaxing, or quiet dinners, as well as a brand new focal point for your house. These long planter boxes can likewise be set on the porch floor to create the illusion of a wall or room divider.

Window boxes can be a visual treat all year round, even during the harshest winters, when boxes can be artfully filled with holly and other evergreens to create a fanciful holiday decoration. Evergreen foliage against a stark white background yields a striking display even in the dead of winter. For another sort of winter box, plant fronds of cabbage palm, trailing green and variegated ivies, and dwarf Lawson's cypress along with some stems of winter cherry (be aware that hard frost may kill off the cabbage palm and winter cherry). Flowering cabbages and kale, densely planted in the window box, add color to the winter porchscape too, and they stand up well to cold temperatures.

Window-box gardening is gardening for pure pleasure. It's not heavy, earth-moving, muscle-straining work and it doesn't require a large financial outlay. A few window boxes on the porch are useful for gardeners who have difficulty with the physical strain of full-scale gardening and provide a compact, easy-to-care-for garden venue for kids too.

Always plant your window boxes using good, enriched soil. Water plants religiously, fertilize frequently, and pinch off spent blooms to encourage new ones, and your window boxes will give you endless hours of enjoyment.

Above: The trailing lobelia and delicate impatiens in both the box and hanging pot are as beautiful to look at as the special fretwork that decorates this porch. The planter box is affixed to the railing well below the line of vision from the porch swing, so as not to disturb the view.

Opposite: The palest flowers and variegated foliage adorn a pair of planter boxes and flow over the edge of hanging pot rims. These delicate plantings are a feminine finishing touch to the wash of pink paint that distinguishes this porch. White and pink gingerbread work, railings, moldings, columns, flowerpots, and flowers match up in nearly perfect choreography to create a playful mood. When we look at this porch, it's almost as if we are peeking in at a movie set.

Hanging Planters

Portulacas, marigolds, and a rainbow of other blooms live in complete harmony on this down-home porch. The sunny yellow paint of vintage high-backed rockers complements the profusion of blooms in this pleasing, albeit crowded, display.

Hang a planter from the ceiling of your porch and you'll add another level of interest. Suspend several planters or baskets and your hanging garden will add a whole new dimension to porch living.

Unlike containers that can be set out in a rather random fashion on the floors and tabletops of your porch, it's important to place hanging planters with care. Take traffic patterns into consideration when deciding on placement, keeping your hanging plants in corners, above porch railings, or in a row, perhaps with ivy trailing low to create a "living wall."

Plantings for the Porch

No matter how lovely a hanging plant looks, it's a nuisance if the pot is placed where people can walk into it. And hanging plants can be quite dangerous if planters are placed in a windy location. Position them only in sheltered spots to avoid losing plants in a storm, not to mention conking someone on the head. And always consider the care and feeding of your hanging plants. Large, airy ferns may look lovely hanging from different levels of a vaulted porch ceiling, but it will be difficult to fertilize and water them. If you have to drag out a ladder every few days to tend to your plants, you may begin avoiding them. It's also harmful for container plants, which require more water and nutrients than plants rooted in the ground, to be hung on the part of the porch that receives direct sun all day. Many of the plants that work best in hanging planters do love the sun, but long days of brightness and heat will exhaust them.

You can either make your own containers for hanging plants using a wire basket, a layer of dried plant material, and enriched soil, or you can buy plants in ready-to-hang containers from a garden center. Either way, they're going to look their best only when they're brimming with abundant, cascading blooms that grow in profusion and cover the sides of the container. In the right location and with lots of attention, these plants will flourish and add living beauty to your porch.

When choosing plants for hanging baskets or pots, consider only the hardiest, bushiest types with a cascading habit, avoiding totally upright, spindly, or finicky types, which will do better planted in the ground.

Always go for the tried and true when planting your hangers and avoid experimentation. Look for petunias, pelargoniums, ivy geraniums, nemesias, portulacas, alyssums, and lobelias. Fuchsias in their many varieties work well, and nasturtiums, ferns, and ivies are also good choices. All these plants trail and arch, creating the best look for a hanging container.

Here are some beautiful hanging-basket combinations to try:

- *white petunias with pale yellow begonias*
- *white lobelia and piggyback plant*
- *light pink begonias with light blue lobelia, vinca, hot pink ivy geraniums, and white alyssum*
- *hot pink fuchsia, piggyback plant, light pink petunias, and silvery helichrysum*

Other Containers

The charming effect of greenery can be readily seen on this tiny back porch, where a few potted ornamental trees take on the stature of a small forest. And the cheerful blooms of impatiens never look so healthy as when they are shielded from the harsh rays of the sun. If you haven't the talent or patience for growing lots of potted plants, don't underestimate the effect you can create with even a single bouquet of fresh flowers. Here, an arrangement of exuberant sunflowers in a florists bucket lends a simple grace to the scene.

There are gardeners, especially those confined to balconies, terraces, and indoor spaces, who plant containers full of everything from petunias and tomatoes to ferns and fig trees. They have learned that container gardening is only as limited as one's imagination. The key, of course, is clever plant selection and appropriate containers.

In the previous two sections, we looked at window boxes and hanging baskets—the workhorses of container planting. In this section, you'll find ideas for other containers, some elegant, others novel, to fill with plants for your porch.

Terra-cotta containers are among the most versatile of vessels. Styled as traditional pots or fashioned with a Mediterranean or Mexican flair, they are universally available in sizes ranging from diminutive to massive. For a romantic, cottagelike flavor, march a row of geranium-filled, matching, terra-cotta flowerpots down the porch stairs. Filling a mismatched collection of terra-cotta with a variety of blooms adds both color and character to a blank corner; to make a bold statement, plant a huge terra-cotta urn with a hibiscus, ficus, or bay tree. Lace it with twinkling lights for evening entertaining.

Cast-cement and reconstituted stone planters also make elegant and versatile containers for porch plants. Many are authentic reproductions of primly plain to profusely ornate antique forms from England, France, and Italy. Exquisitely detailed cast-lead planters are also being made, some from the original molds. Look for them at high-quality garden centers and at dealers who specialize in garden ornaments.

Fifties-style pastel flowerpots look wonderful overflowing with mixes of green houseplants like philodendron, ferns, fittonia, prayer plant, croton, burro's tail, tiger aloc, or seersucker plant, which provide contrasting textures. Porcelain and ceramic pottery, too, are available in a range of designs and colors, and add a somewhat more refined air to the space.

A collection of baskets can find useful lives as cache pots for planters of colorful, sun-loving annuals like marigolds, ageratum, geraniums, nicotianas, calendulas, and portulacas.

Casual summertime living is here at its best. Huge expanses of glass are fitted with sliding doors, allowing access to the long sweep of porch from all rooms. A pair of potted tropical plants stands guard on either side of a large window, balancing the seating area on the one side and the tree on the other. Containerized trees and shrubs, as well as large plants like these, can bring visual weight and balance to a setting less expensively than additional furniture.

A modest entrance blooms with the beauty of lush, colorful flowers in attractive terra-cotta and stone pots. Container plants will flourish and provide much enjoyment if they are watered and fed regularly and spent blooms removed. Granite finials in a stylized pineapple design rest at the very bottom of the stairs, trumpeting a welcome to all who visit.

Scour yard sales, flea markets, and tag sales for vintage brass, copper, or enameled pots, which make attractive containers for both flowers and greenery. An old milk bucket, washtub, or feed trough crammed with annuals provides instant charm to a porch garden, as do old-fashioned wooden shipping crates or a small child's wagon.

If summer cooking is your passion, fill strawberry jars with culinary herbs like parsley, thyme, rosemary, tarragon, sage, and chives. Put them in a sunny spot on the back porch so you'll have them handy when you're preparing your nightly feasts.

You don't have to limit your container growing to flowers and herbs. Many porch gardeners have had horticultural triumphs with container-grown vegetables. And seed companies have been quick to respond to the needs of small-space gardeners with dwarf and vining varieties that do well in pots.

When you cluster a group of containers, be sure to vary the sizes and shapes—a tall narrow pot anchored by three short, squat containers is more effective than three or four pots all of a size. And keep in mind that, like in garden planting, groups of three or more usually look better than just two.

Try to see a link between the containers you use and the style of your porch. The clean lines of a contemporary beach house porch are beautifully complemented by large, square, white-painted wooden planters that proudly display bushy sky blue hydrangeas or standards of sunny marguerites. Lacy wire and wicker plant stands boasting lush ferns make a Victorian porch come alive, while buckets, baskets, and pottery bursting with colorful blooms add immeasurably to a simple cottage porch.

To keep container plants happy, use a good, all-purpose fertilizer. Water-soluble types are probably the easiest to use because you simply dissolve the fertilizer in a watering can and apply it to plants during regular watering.

If you live in an area where winter temperatures drop below freezing, you'll need to take a few precautions with certain kinds of containers. Terra-cotta pots should be emptied, cleaned, and dried thoroughly, then stored in a dry place for the cold season. If pots are wet when they freeze, they will crack. Cement and reconstituted stone planters are less vulnerable to damage from freezing, but you can extend the life of your favorite ones by storing them away from the elements too. Reproduction lead pieces and planters made of redwood are designed to stand up to the elements, however, cleaning and dry storage of any planter certainly wouldn't hurt. It amounts to old-fashioned good porch-keeping!

Almost picture perfect, this tiny portico is wreathed in wonderfully scented climbing roses. While roses aren't true vines, and therefore need some encouragement to clamber, they'll happily train over an arch, up a wall, or around a column as long as they are supported with ties. While greeting you each day with their delicate blossoms and classic perfume, the more free-flowering climbing rose cultivars also provide enough blooms for indoor arrangements.

Leafy Bowers

Natural shade, cast by the shadows of a tree or a vine that has been trained to climb up a trellis or porch railing, can help make your porch a special place. If you want to avoid using shades or drapery to block or filter sunlight, it's important to create a landscape plan that includes natural screens or living curtains in all the right places.

The first thing you'll need to do is take note of the path of the sun throughout the day, observing how it brightens your porch. Consider the best places on your property to site trees that will provide the shade you need. You'll also want to think about the impact of this shade on other parts of your property, where sun-loving perennials and vegetables may be growing. Take all angles into consideration and look for deciduous trees (those that lose their leaves in the fall) or evergreens that are relatively fast growers. You won't want to wait eight to ten years for your shade. Among the fastest-growing deciduous varieties are red maple, green ash, American sycamore (though some find it undesirable because of the continually peeling bark), English oak, bald cypress, linden, and Bradford pear. Evergreen choices include white pine, Norway spruce, and eastern arborvitae.

Note, though, that tall evergreens growing too close to the house may provide pleasant coolness and shade on your porch in the summer, but in a harsh, snowy winter the interior of your house could take on a cold and dismal atmosphere. If your porch has a southern exposure, deciduous trees are the best choices. They offer shade in the summer and allow the sun to penetrate in the winter. Take all these things into consideration before you plant, and if you're working with a landscape designer, be sure to communicate all your concerns before he or she begins to develop a plan.

Mature trees add a touch of magnificence to this property, providing the yard and porch with plenty of natural shade. Planning for shade trees is a long-range project, since they will take years to mature, but is well worth the effort if you love the coolness of a wooded area. Here, the liberal use of colorful annuals in planter boxes and in the handsome circular bed provide bright focal points.

Plantings for the Porch

A view of a country garden from a shady, quiet porch can work wonders for jangled nerves. Foliage trailing from a hanging planter links the man-made porch to its more natural surroundings. Evening shadows have lengthened across this porch, signaling the perfect hour for enjoying an iced drink or a light supper.

Leafy vines, many of which die back in the winter months, offer a perfect—and much faster-growing—alternative to shade trees. Consider Boston ivy, wisteria, sweet autumn clematis, silver lace vine, and honeysuckle, all of which are fast-growing vines that can be trained to travel up porch posts, across railings, and on trellises. In warm climates you might try Carolina jasmine, star jasmine, Persian ivy, or a yellow, vining form of bleeding heart called *Dicentra scandens*.

Annual vines can also be fast growing and will provide you with a cooling, leafy bower in a matter of weeks. Try morning glories, hops, marble vine, hyacinth bean, scarlet runner bean, or balsam pear.

Foundation Plantings

It's amazing how a few well-chosen shrubs placed correctly and imaginatively will enhance the setting of your porch and hide exposed concrete, latticework, and support posts, which can detract from the overall beauty of your home. Subtle differences in plant size, form, color, and texture will provide harmony and balance and unify your house and garden.

If your porch is a brand-new addition to your home, or if you've just completed a porch restoration, this might be the perfect time to rethink your landscape design entirely. You now have the opportunity to capitalize on the new look your porch has given your home. If you decide to showcase your porch with new plantings, realize that they may not blend all that well with the existing landscaping scheme. In this case, you'll need to spend some time at the drawing board. Consult with a landscape professional to devise a new plan if you don't feel confident about doing it yourself or if you don't have the time or the inclination to adequately research different types of plantings.

Foundation plantings must blend with the rest of your landscape if they are to provide the finished look that is their assigned role. Designing a landscape is an art that requires knowledge and the ability to make the best use of available space in the most attractive way. It means shaping the land to beautify your property, and since it can be a major investment, selecting plants that fit the design is key.

It's essential to work from a master plan, but landscaping can be completed in stages if it's prohibitively expensive or time-consuming to do all at once. Your site must be examined from all angles with an eye toward maximizing use and minimizing upkeep. It may take several years to implement your design but without a plan, costly mistakes can occur.

Multiple levels of porches, stairways, and railings make for interesting architectural detailing, but create a challenging scenario for a landscaper. A barrage of hanging planters, vines, and flower boxes would only create a detrimental busyness and draw attention away from the lovely design details in the balustrades and the spindlework along the top of the porch. Instead, the dark, cool greens of a bushy hibiscus and a well-placed tree complement the porch beautifully, making pristine whites even brighter.

The magnificent thicket of rosebushes surrounding this old-fashioned wraparound porch appears to be as solid and permanent as any feature of this small but charming home. All shades of pink and red as well as white and yellow grace the extravagantly wide border, which features climbing roses twining up the porch columns and miniatures underplanted below the hedge roses. Glorious scents waft over the porch and through the house on still, somewhat humid, afternoons.

The best selections for foundation plantings are slow-growing varieties that retain interest throughout the year. Evergreens, either the broad-leafed or needle varieties, are good choices, but do your research and use care in making selections if you are doing your own landscaping. A Colorado or Norway spruce that can grow thirty feet or higher will cast deep shade on the porch area and other parts of the house, causing dampness and possibly mold or mildew on exterior walls. Such a tree will also shade interior rooms in winter, giving them a dank, gloomy look.

The best foundation plants are slow growers that don't require great amounts of care and pruning. Yews, viburnum, cotoneasters, holly, rhododendrons, azaleas, potentillas, spireas, and barberries are good choices. With a little careful planning, you can satisfy all your porch and landscape dreams

FURTHER READING

Best Home Plans: Indoor/Outdoor Living. Menlo Park, California: Sunset Publishing Corp., 1993.

Buchanan, George. *Garden Furniture: A Practical Handbook for Woodworkers.* London: Ward Lock, 1991

Davidson, Myra. *Pillows, Curtains & More.* Chilton, 1993.

Editors of Time-Life Books. *Curtains & Shades.* Alexandria, Virginia: Time-Life Books, 1985.

Fleming, John, Hugh Honour, and Nicholaus Pevsner. *Dictionary of Architecture.* New York: Penguin Books, 1991.

Hirschman, Jessica Elin. *For Your Home: Porches & Sunrooms.* Boston: Little, Brown and Company, 1993.

Kahn, Renee and Ellen Meagher. *Preserving Porches.* New York: Henry Holt and Company, 1984.

Robbins, Sally Fennell. *Porch Presence: Interior Design for the Exterior Room.* New York: Friedman/Fairfax Publishers, 1995.

Thomerson, Carole. *The Complete Upholsterer: A Practical Guide to Upholstering Traditional Furniture.* New York: Alfred A. Knopf, Inc., 1989.

Wissinger, Joanna. *Victorian Details: Enhancing Antique and Contemporary Homes with Period Accents.* New York: E.P. Dutton, 1990.

Zingman-Leith, Elan and Susan Zingman-Leith. *The Secret Life of Victorian Houses.* Washington, DC: Elliott & Clark Publishing, 1993.

SOURCES

Restoration and Preservation

Anthony Wood Products Inc.
Box 1081x
Hillsboro, TX 76645
(817) 582-7225
Specializing in Victorian gingerbread.

Chadsworth Inc.
PO Box 53268
Atlanta, GA 30355
(404) 876-5410
Manufacturer of classical colulmns and capitals for porches and porticos.

Oehrlein & Associates
Architects
1702 Connecticut Ave., NW
Washington, DC 20009
(202) 387-8040
Technical consulting, architectural design and restoration advice.

Society for the Preservation of New England Antiquities
185 Lyman St.
Waltham, MA 02154
(617) 891-1985
Technical advice no matter where you live.

Traditional Line Ltd.,
Architectural Restoration
143 W. 21st St.
New York, NY 10011
(212) 627-3555
Architectural restoration.

Furnishings

The Astrup Company
2937 W. 25th St.
Cleveland,OH 44113
(216) 696-2820
Traditional awnings and hardware for over 115 years.

Bielecky Bros. Wicker Furniture
306 East 61st St.
New York, NY 10021
(212) 735-2355
Wicker, rattan, and cane furniture.

Blake Industries
PO Box 155
Abington,MA 02351
(617) 337-8772
Cast-iron and wood reproduction park benches.

Brandywine Garden Furniture
24 Phoenixville Pike
Malvern, PA 19355
(800) 725-5435
Teak and hardwood garden furniture, including benches, chairs, tables, tea carts and planters.

Chandlertown Chairworks
PO Box 1630
Chandler, NC 28715
(704) 667-4844
Country furniture including chairs, rockers and a red oak swing.

Devenco Louver Products
PO Box 700
Decatur, GA 30031
(404) 378-4597
Custom-made wooden-slat Venetian blinds and old-fashioned wooden porch shades.

Green Enterpirses
43 Rogers St.
Hamilton, VA 22068
(703) 338-3606
Reproduction Victorian benches, chairs, swings, gliders, etc.

Lawler Machine and Foundry Co.
PO Box 320069
Birmingham, AL 35232
(205) 595-0596
Simple cast-iron ended, wooden-seated porch swings.

Lineal Design
6142 15th St. East
Bradenton, FL 34203
Quality aluminum casual furniture.

Lloyd/Flanders
3010 Tenth St.
Menominee, MI
(906) 863-4491
Wicker furniture since 1906.

MDT-Muller Design, Inc.
971 Dogwood Trail
Tyrone, GA 30290
(404) 631-9074
Umbrellas.

The Old Wagon Factory
103 Russell St.
Clarksville, VA 23927
(804) 374-5787
Classic wood porch furniture with Chippendale details.

The Outdoor Lamp Company
6307 Ridge Road
Port Richey, FL 34668
(800) 535-3411
Outdoor lighting.

Pacific Rattan
Harbour Towne
201 Samsonite Blvd.
Murfreesboro, TN 37129
(615) 893-0300
Rattan and wicker furniture.

Pompeian Studios
90 Rockledge Road
Bronxville, NY 10708-5208
(800) 457-5595
Wrought-iron tables, chairs, consoles, settees, gliders, etc., hand-forged in Italy.

Shaker Workshops
PO Box 1028
Concord, MA 01742
(617) 646-8985
Traditional Shaker rockers, chairs, and tables.

Tennessee Fabricating
Company
1822 Latham St.
Memphis, TN 38106
(901) 948-3356
Ornamental outdoor furniture including settees,tables, benches, and chairs.

Universal Gloster Inc.
1555-57 Carmen Dr.
Elk Grove Village, IL 60007
(708) 362-9400
Teak outdoor furniture in traditional English and innovative designs.

Vermont Outdoor Furniture
East Barre, VT 05649
(800) 588-8834
Mail-order northern white cedar benches, chairs, tables, etc.

Wicker Cottage
PO Box 42274
Houston, TX 77242
(713) 781-0678
Wicker furniture.

Wicker by Henry Link
Lexington Furniture Industries
Lexington, NC 27293
Wicker for indoor and out door use.

Woodard
317 South Elm St.
Owosso, MI 48867
(517) 725-2290
Wrought-iron furniture.

Greenhouses and Conservatories

Amdega Conservatories
Boston Design Center
1 Design Center Plaza
Suite 624
Boston, MA 02210
(617) 951 2755
An English firm specializing in Victorian conservatories.

Sturdi-built Greenhouse
Manufacturing Company
Dept. F
11304 SW Boones Ferry Road
Portland, OR 97219
(800) 722-4115
Greenhouse, sunroom, garden room designs.

Sun Room Company, Inc.
322 E. Main St.
Leola, PA 17540
(800) 426-0843
Victorian, lean-to, and custom sunrooms.

Sources

Plants, Pots, and Other Gardening Needs

Architectural Brick Paving Ltd.
Department 384
1187 Wilmette Ave.
Wlmette, IL 60091
(708) 256-8432
  Adaptations of trellising and other architectural elements from antiquity to the Renaissance.

The Fragrant Path
PO Box 328
Fort Calhoun, NE 68023
  Mail-order seeds for fragrant, rare, and old-fashioned plants.

Gardener's Eden
PO Box 7307
San Francisco, CA 94120-7307
(415) 421-4242
  Mail-order gardening supplies.

Kenneth Lynch and Sons
78 Danbury Road
Wilton, CT 06897-0488
(203) 7620-8363
  More than fifty styles of cast stone or fiberglass planters.

Smith & Hawkin
25 Corte Madera
Mill Valley, CA 94941
(415) 383-2000
  Mail-order gardening supplies.

Thompson & Morgan
PO Box 1308
Jackson, NJ 08527
(908) 363-2225
(800) 274-7333 (outside New Jersey)
  Mail-order seeds for flowers and vegetables.

Valcovic Cornell Design
Box 380
Beverly, MA 01915
  Sculptured trellises from a catalog.

Wayside Gardens
1 Garden Lane
Hodges, SC 29695-0001
(800) 845-1124
  Mail-order plants, including shrubs, trees, roses, and perennials.

White Flower Farm
Litchfield, CT 16759-0050
(203) 496-9600
  Mail-order plants, including shrubs, roses, and perennials; tools and containers, including unusual terra rossa pots and planters.

W. Atlee Burpee & Company
300 Park Avenue
Warminster, PA 18991-0003
(800) 888-1447
  Mail-order flower, herb, and vegetable seeds and plants.

Australian Sources

Country Farm Perennials
RSD Laings Road
Nayook VIC 3821

Design Warehouse
Cromo Toorak Road
South Yarra, Victoria 3141
Melbourne

Honeysuckle Cottage Nursery
Lot 35 Bowen Mountain Road
Bown Mountain via
Grosevale, NSW 2753

Remo Mail Order Catalog
Oxford at Crown Street
Sydney

Canadian Sources

Au Courant
1200 Queen Street East
Toronto, Ontario M4M 1K8

Ferncliff Gardens
SS1
Mission, British Columbia
V2V 5V6

McFayden Seed Co. Ltd.
Box 1800
Brandon, Manitoba
R7A 6N4

Quintessence Designs
1222 Young Street
Toronto, Ontario M40 1W3

PHOTOGRAPHY CREDITS

© Peter Aaron/Esto: 36 left, 38, 82, 117

© William Abranowicz: 20, 39, 88, 102, 103

© Otto Baitz/Esto: 40, 72, 80

© Corbis-Bettmann: 13

© Mark Darley/Esto: 50–51, 65

© Elizabeth Whiting Associates: 6, 7, 8–9

© Philip Ennis: 105 (designed by Gail and Stephen Huberman)

© Feliciano: 70, 98 (designed by Lyn Petersen), 121

© Andrew Garn: 77, 87, 99

© Nancy Hill: 16, 44, 45 (designed by Stephanie Stokes), 58 (designed by Jan Burkett), 60, 125, 126

© image/dennis krukowski: 24, 74, 120; Design: Antony Childs, Inc.: 79; Design: Bunny Williams Inc.: 93 right, 104; Design: Gary Crain Inc.: 89, 106; Design: Ron Grimaldi of Rose Cummings, Inc.: 46–47, 55; Design: Iron Horse Vineyards: 54; Design: Jean P. Simmers, Ltd. Interior Design: 118; Design: John Saladino, Inc.: 84 right; Design: Mandrake: 96; Design: Paul Leonard Design Associates, Inc. and Regine A. Laverge, Paris Garden Arts: 57, 62–63; Design: Peabody Clark: 76 right; Design: Robert Decarlo Design Associates: 10; Design: Robert Metzger Inc., Michael Christiano Associate: 59; Design: Rolf Seckinger and Associates, Inc.: 52, 115; Design: Shelly Rosenberg Design Studio: 66, Design: Tonin MacCallum A.S.I.D., Inc.: 108, 112–113, 116, 139

© Jessie Walker Associates: 12 top, 67, 110, 134

© Balthazar Korab: 14 left, 19 right, 76 left, 84 left, 131, 138

© David Livingston: 3 (William Turnbull Associates), 36 right, 92–93 (designed by Sharon Campbell)

© Charles Mann: 141 (courtesy Mike Shoup Antique Rose Emporium)

© Peter Mauss/Esto: 31, 32, 37

© David Phelps: 42 (courtesy *American Homestyle & Gardening* magazine), 64, 85 (courtesy *Womans Day* specials, designed by Charles Riley), 137 (courtesy *American Homestyle & Gardening* magazine, designed by Max King)

© Paul Rocheleau: 9 right, 14 right, 15, 26 bottom, 47 right, 140

© Eric Roth: 23, 49 right (Captain Farris House, South Yarmouth, MA), 56 right (designed by Carole Kaplan from Two By Two Interior Design), 68 (Robert Miklos, principal architect, Schwartz/Silver Architects), 100 (designed by Holly McGowan, Coastal Design), 111 (courtesy of L.L. Bean), 113 right, 114 left, 114 right (Captain Farris House), 119 (Betsy Brown Landscape Design), 124, 130, 132, 134 (designed by Paul Magnuson), 136 (Betsy Brown Landscape Design)

© Keith Scott Morton: 48, 83

© Joe Standart: 2, 11, 61, 73, 81, 109

© Tim Street-Porter: 12 bottom, 63 right (designed by Tom Callaway), 69 (designed by Paulene Morton), 71 (John Woolf Architect), 75 (designed by Jarrett Hedborg, wall painting by Nancy Kintisch), 90 (designed by Michael Anderson), 95, 122 (designed by Tom Callaway), 123 (designed by Kate Stamps), 129, 135 (designed by Jarrett Hedborg)

© Brian Vanden Brink: 1, 17, 18–19, 21 (built by Bullock & Co.), 22 (courtesy Delamater House, Rhinebeck, NY), 25 (courtesy Inn by the Sea, Portland, ME), 26 top (Steven Foote Architect), 27 (Winton Scott Architect), 28–29 (Smith Alvarez Sienkiewycz Architects), 33, 41 (Rob Whitten Architect), 49 left (Jack Silverio Architect), 53, 86, 101

© Paul Warchol: 30 (Margaret Helfand Architect), 35 (Haverson Architecture), 43 (designed by David Coleman Architecture)

Index